T0354478

YOU CAN'T MAKE THIS ~~STUFF~~ ~~SHIT~~ UP

JAY LASZLOW PORTER

iUniverse

YOU CAN'T MAKE THIS STUFF UP

iUniverse books may be ordered through booksellers or by contacting:

iUniverse
1663 Liberty Drive
Bloomington, IN 47403
www.iuniverse.com
1-800-Authors (1-800-288-4677)

Because of the dynamic nature of the Internet, any web addresses or links contained in this book may have changed since publication and may no longer be valid. The views expressed in this work are solely those of the author and do not necessarily reflect the views of the publisher, and the publisher hereby disclaims any responsibility for them.

Any people depicted in stock imagery provided by Getty Images are models, and such images are being used for illustrative purposes only. Certain stock imagery © Getty Images.

ISBN: 978-1-5320-8234-4 (sc)
ISBN: 978-1-5320-8233-7 (e)

Library of Congress Control Number: 2019914367

Print information available on the last page.

iUniverse rev. date: 10/15/2019

CONTENTS

DEDICATION

This book is dedicated to my wife, who has been with me for most of my life. She has patiently and tirelessly endured most of the events that are described here (including hearing me repeat them to her for this book).

I also dedicate this book to my children and grandchildren, who have heard many of these stories more times than they would like.

PROLOGUE

Most of the stories in this book are those that occurred throughout my life, with my personal slant included. I also added a few stories that have been told to me by others over the years.

I recently retired, and I had the time to write these stories down. At least as many as I can remember (memory may not my best trait anymore).

Often, someone said something that triggered my long-term memory (that seems to still work). I wrote down a note with keywords so I wouldn't forget the gist, and then I added a story to this book. I've included approximately 250 such stories.

The names and places in my stories have been removed to protect the innocent, but hopefully I've saved the essence of each one.

Several years before I retired, I realized that everything can be related to 1 simple rule.

Rule #1: **You can't make this stuff up.**

I said this a lot at work. My colleagues laughed each time, but they always commented that I say it.

Things always seem to follow this pattern.

This book is divided into 11 categories, as shown in the Contents.

See if you agree that Rule #1 applies to most (if not all) of these stories.

My hope is that you will enjoy these stories as much as I did when I experienced them.

CATEGORY 1

MY CHILDHOOD
AND COLLEGE

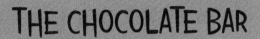

THE CHOCOLATE BAR

When I was 5 years old, we went to my grandparents' place for dinner.

Everyone was downstairs, and after dinner, I was bored. So I went exploring upstairs, as a 5-year-old boy will do.

I rummaged through my grandparents' drawers and found a chocolate bar.

Good thing for a 5-year-old to find, right?

I ate it.

It turned out to be "Ex-Lax."

I spent the rest of the day on the pot.

Not pretty.

What does a 5-year-old know?

PLAYING POOL

When I was in high school, one of my cool friends asked me if I played pool. Wanting to be cool too, I said that I did. My dad had bought me a small (five feet long) pool table, and I played pool on it in the basement.

"Why don't we go to a billiards place and shoot a few games?" he asked.

"Sure," I said, still trying to act cool.

We went to a local billiards place. It was in the basement of a bowling alley. There were many tables, all nine feet long. The big ones. Each table had three shaded lamps above its playing surface. The rest of the place was dark. It looked very sleazy.

We played a game, and I won. Then he asked me if I wanted to play some games for a dollar each. Loser would pay for the time of the table, out of his losses. Still trying to act cool, I agreed.

After we split a few games, he was up two dollars. Shall we raise it to two dollars a game? Sure, I said again. Then we raised it to four dollars a game.

I had no idea what he was doing.

But at four dollars a game, the pressure became amplified. He won a game. Then I hit a lucky shot and won a game. Back and forth. Finally, he was up two games, or eight dollars.

I realized that I was being bustled, and I said I had enough. I paid for the time. We had been there so long that the time cost $7.60. I gave him the difference. Forty cents.

I never fell for being hustled again!

But I was cool! At least for several hours.

THE HOAGIE LADY

When I started college, I met a few classmates and we began going to lunch together in the Cafeteria. I quickly decided that the best lunch was a hoagie. So I ordered it from the same little old lady. Every day.

The little old lady was very nice. She was short, and she wore her gray hair in a bun with a net around it. She also had a mole on the left side of her chin, and there was a hair sticking out of the mole. You couldn't help but notice it.

So one day, we approached the little old lady at her sandwich station. Before I could order my usual hoagie, the little old lady said that she had to go in the back to get more deli ingredients for the hoagies.

When she came out, she was carrying three tall piles of deli: Italian ham on the right, prosciutto in the middle, and provolone cheese on the left. The piles were so tall that she had to lean back and carry them against her body, with her arms at the bottom.

To stabilize the piles, the little old lady placed her chin on top. When I saw her doing this, the mole and the little hair were stuck in the top of the pile of provolone cheese.

She put the ingredients in the containers on the counter and went back to her sandwich station. Then she said, "What can I get for you?"

I said, "Could I have a hot dog?"

THE ROTC RIFLE

In college, I took ROTC (Reserve Officers Training Corps). I attended class two days a week. After the classes, on another day, we had drill. For drill, we had to put on our uniform, get our rifle from the storage facility, and then get out to the field and drill for an hour, no matter what the weather.

After drill, you had to return your rifle.

On a day between classes and drill, based on my schedule, I had a few hours. I was playing cards in the Activities Center with several friends. We were in our uniforms, and we had already picked up our rifles. They were against the wall, where we could all keep an eye on them.

When it was time to drill, everyone took their rifle and headed for the field. After the drill, I returned my rifle to the storage facility, and then I went back to the Activities Center.

There was one of my friends, still playing cards with some other students, with his rifle against the wall.

When my friend finally remembered to return his rifle, the storage facility was closed.

The FBI had been notified when his rifle wasn't returned in time. They were looking for my friend and his rifle.

My friend was punished severely.

I thought they would expel him!

He left college instead.

MY FIRST CO-OP JOB

I went to a college that included co-op jobs. That way you could get on-the-job training (OJT) before you graduated. I wanted that as part of my college experience.

At the end of my first year, I was assigned my first co-op job. It was out of state. I had two assignments there.

They had several departments, including one department that had so much business that it needed its own secretary.

The secretary was tall and had a perfect figure. However, she just wasn't that pretty.

When I first met her, I asked her, "What do they call you?"

She said to me, "I don't care what they call me, as long as they call me."

THE LAB CABINET

To get my college degree, I had four co-op assignments at two different companies, for the OJT experience.

My second pair of assignments was in a test lab, testing material properties of metals.

The lab was a large rectangular room, with a smaller anteroom attached to the side for the office of the lab supervisor. Both rooms opened to the same main hallway.

I got to know all of the people in the lab, and also the engineers of the group who worked down the main hallway. The manager down the hall was in charge of both the engineers and the lab. His secretary sat outside his office. She was a very pretty brunette. Long hair, beautiful figure, 5'8" in heels.

She liked one of the test guys in the lab, and she stopped in one day to visit him. This was, of course, against company policy. So she did this on the sly.

When she was there, all of us in the lab heard the manager's voice, as he stopped in the anteroom to speak with the supervisor.

The secretary wanted to hide, since she couldn't be found in the lab, where she wasn't supposed to be. She went to a 6-foot metal cabinet, opened its door, and slid inside. The cabinet was tall enough that she could fit. Then she closed the door to hide.

As luck would have it, that's exactly where the manager was going. He opened the door to the metal cabinet, and there stood his secretary.

She waved at the manager and smiled.

"Hi," she said.

THE PLOTTER

In the test lab, the supervisor was good at fixing the electronic equipment. There was an X-Y plotter (an archaic way of plotting, available at the time) that wasn't working properly.

So he disassembled the plotter and then had all the gears, sprockets, wires, nuts and bolts lying on the floor. After several hours, he reassembled the plotter, but it still wouldn't work.

Just then the manager walked in and saw what the supervisor was working on.

"Can't get this darned plotter to work," the supervisor grumbled.

The manager looked around and then he said, "Why don't you plug it in?"

It was unplugged.

The supervisor plugged it in and it worked. I guess he put it back together properly.

We all had a good laugh.

Since then, I've always checked to see if something is plugged in before I go any farther.

THE LAB TECHS

During my second assignment in the test lab, I became friendly with one of the lab techs. He was a real character.

One day he came into the lab wearing a neck brace.

"What happened to you?" I heard someone ask.

"I dove into a swimming pool. The problem was that it was empty."

One of the other lab techs invited me and my girlfriend (later to be my wife) to his house for dinner. His wife and two young blond-haired boys were there.

Dinner was delightful. We had appetizers and then the main course. When the boys were eating the main course, one of them didn't feel well. In fact, he felt so bad that he threw up right there at the dinner table.

I guess the lab tech was used to this with his two boys. While he continued eating his main course, he reached out and caught the droppings from his son's mouth!

My wife and I have been married for over 50 years. She still remembers the event clearly. What surprised me was that in spite of what she witnessed that night, we still had two children.

THE ARMY PHYSICAL

When I was a junior, my college made a mistake and sent the wrong information to the Selective Service Board. I received a 1A (draftable) classification in the mail. I should have been 2S (student, not draftable). My mother opened the letter while I was in school, and she had it corrected before I got home. After she had 2 coronaries.

However, I still had to take the army physical. The appointment was a week later at 8:00 AM.

I arrived at the appointed time, and the first item was a written test. It took about an hour. Then I went through the processing. I had to remove clothing down to my shorts and socks. Then I went to the weighing scale.

I stepped on the analog scale and the needle went way up to 195 pounds. Then it settled at around 155 pounds, my weight. The sergeant read my weight when the needle hit maximum, as 195 pounds!

"Hey!" I exclaimed.

Then he jammed the height measuring bar down on my head, forcing me to bend down. The measuring bar followed me down.

He said, "5'4" tall." I was 5'9" tall.

So in the army records, I'm listed as 5'4" tall, 195 pounds. I'm a fireplug.

Next was my vision check. The sergeant told me to remove my glasses and look in the device, then read the chart.

I took off my glasses and looked in the device. All I saw was a bright light at a distance. "I can't see anything."

"Just read the chart," he grumbled.

"Let me put on my glasses." I put them on and saw that the device had lenses to make the chart appear farther away. I read the chart. He wrote something down.

Next I was led to a long bench, where I sat in my shorts and socks. There were more than 20 people in front of me. They were calling 10 at a time. When each group of ten was called, the rest of us had to slide down the bench. That meant that if any of the guys before me were sweating on the bench, my right thigh would pick up their secretions. Yuck!!

I finally got near the end of the bench, and then they called the next 10 guys to go around the corner. I was third. We stood in a line, and the guy wearing a white robe said, "Drop your shorts, turn around and bend over. When I tap you on the back, stand up and turn around."

When he tapped me on the back I stood up and turned around. Then he got to the fifth guy. "How long have you had this problem?" he asked rather loudly.

The first four of us were already standing, and we looked intently to see what the fifth guy's problem was. He had *boils*. Yuck!!

White robe finished the line and then put on a plastic glove. He then went to the first guy and checked him for a hernia. Finger under his scrotum, pushing up. Then he said, "Cough." He went to the second guy. Same deal. When he got to me, I said, "Would you mind changing your glove?"

He grumbled, but he changed his glove.

Then he pushed his finger under my scrotum really hard. I went up on my toes, but that didn't help. He just pushed farther.

I was on my toes, impaled.

Then he said, "Cough."

I couldn't.

He finally removed his finger. I was so relieved.

He moved on to the last 7 guys, and I can't remember if he changed his glove for them.

After that was over, we were finished. I got dressed and went to get my morning test score. The test conductor said that you needed 14 to pass. Out of what? I thought. Turned out it was out of 100! My score was in the 90s.

It was now 12:30 PM.

The test conductor said, "The following 3 guys didn't pass." He read their names. Then he said, "You'll take the test until you do pass. Follow me."

So those 3 guys had to re-take the test until they scored a 14 and passed!

The test was multiple choice, and you had to pick from A, B, C, D and E. Even if you picked all "A" answers, on average you should get a 20!

I guess the army is used to people purposely failing their test scores so they can try to avoid being drafted.

The army found a way around that!

The entire process was demeaning. I was delighted when it was over.

THE MIRACLE

When I went to college, I chose a program with co-op jobs for OJT. I goofed off in my first two years, and at the end of my sophomore year, my cumulative grade point average was 71.1.

You needed a 70.0 to stay in school.

I was barely hanging in there.

My college decided to go onto the 4.0 (ABC) grading system, where the students would receive either A, B, C, D, or F for the course grade, used to calculate a student's Grade Point Average (GPA).

The new freshmen were on the 4.0 system. Old freshmen becoming sophomores had their grades converted to the 4.0 system. The juniors becoming seniors finished their degrees on the numerical system. My group was the sophomores becoming juniors. The school decided to freeze our numerical grades, and we would start fresh on the 4.0 system.

This was definitely a miracle.

Fortunately, I realized that I had been given a second chance.

I was on the Dean's list for my last 2 years, with a 3.62 GPA for those 2 years. I also learned the stuff from previous years that I'd missed.

I graduated and went to work. While working I achieved a Masters' degree and a PhD. My division was sold off, but other than 2 short stints at neighboring facilities, I continued in the same place throughout my career. I ended my 50-year career as a company Fellow.

I never let my kids pull any of the stuff I did. That's why they're successful.

CATEGORY 2

FAMILY

MY MOTHER'S AGE

When my mother met my father, he told her he was 36. She told him she was 35.

We don't know if she were older than my father or not, but we know for sure that it was better that she told him she was younger.

Her birthday was either February 12 or June 1. She wasn't sure. We always celebrated it on February 12.

It gave fuel to the question about her age.

On February 12, 1995, after my father passed, we threw a 90th birthday party for my mother at a very good local Italian restaurant.
My mother never had a birthday party to mark a previous major birthday, and she was delighted.

She died at when she was almost 92. She still never told us how old she really was.

MOTHER

When my mother and father got married, my mother was 36 (at least that's what everyone believed) and my father was 37.

A month after my mother turned 38, she didn't feel well, so she went to the family doctor, an allergist by specialty.

After his examination, he told my mother that she was pregnant, but he could take care of it if she wanted.

"No," she calmly said. "My husband doesn't have any children. He'll love this."

I was born later in the year.

When I was about 15 years old, my mother told me the story of how she found out she was pregnant. After I heard it, I never liked that doctor anymore.

He was talking about getting rid of *me*!

DINNER AT HER PARENTS' HOUSE

When I was still 16, I had dinner at my girlfriend's house (later to be my wife). Her mother asked if I wanted a steak or lamb chops.

I said, "I'd like a steak, if it's not too much trouble."

"How do you like it cooked?"

"I like it rare."

"Cannibal!" she exclaimed.

I should have heard the warning in her voice, but still I continued. "I can tell when it's done by the smell coming out of the oven."

Gasoline on a raging fire.

"Okay," she said. But she gave me a look.

Her mother threw several steaks in the oven, and the cooking began.

Then a wonderful aroma billowed from the oven.

I said, "It smells great. It's ready!"

"Not yet," she replied.

The cooking continued. And continued.

As I looked on helplessly.

When her mother served the steak, it went "clunk" on my plate.

What made this memorable was that her father's steak was well done!

FLUSH YOUR KIDNEYS

One of my wife's uncles was a real character. He had lots of sayings, but the thing I remember about him the most was that he was always saying, "Drink a lot of water. Flush your kidneys."

I didn't think much of it. But as I got older, I began to get kidney stones. I remember when my doctor told me, "You're an active former."

"I am *not!*" I replied.

But I guess I was. I've had a total of 6 kidney stones over the years.

It's not pleasant. Women have told me that it's like giving birth, but not as painful.

If kidney stones are really not as painful, then childbirth is out of the question for me.

I drink a lot of water now. Who knew that her uncle was right all along?

BASEBALL QUIZ

In 1964, we had dinner reservations for Father's Day at a restaurant, but my dad refused to leave until he saw the end of the Phillies' baseball game. It was when Jim Bunning was pitching a perfect game (27 straight outs in a 9-inning game).

My dad saw it to the end.

He even talked about the perfect game with the people at the next table in the restaurant, much to my mother's disgust.

So one day, we had the family at our house, and our nephew was there. He was 12 years old. We were talking about my dad being a baseball expert. When our nephew heard that my father stayed to watch the end of Jim Bunning's perfect game, he asked my dad, "Can I try to trip you up with a question?"

"Sure," my dad replied.

"Who pitched the only perfect game in the World Series?" our nephew asked. An appropriate question.

"That's too easy," my dad said. "It was Don Larsen in 1956. But the right question is, 'Who was the umpire?'"

"*Umpire?*" our nephew said completely exasperated. "Who cares about the *umpire!*"

"It was Babe Pinelli. And the reason why it's important is that the 27th out was a called third strike."

Our nephew grumbled, but he didn't ask any more questions.

OuR WEDDING

My wife and I were getting married. It was a typical June wedding. I was all dressed, with a white jacket and black pants. It was the tux of the season.

As I was leaving to drive to the venue, I reached for my car door and a bird flying by pooped on my hand. Missed the white jacket completely.

Good luck? Must have been.

We're married over 50 years!

As I was readying to go down the aisle, my father-in-law to be turned to me and started a tradition. He said, "It's not too late. You can back out, and we'll have a great party. But if you go through with this, I never want to hear about it again."

Scared the hell out of me, but I proceeded on.

He never did hear about it again from me!

THE TRADITION

I passed on the tradition that my father-in-law gave me at my wedding, telling me that I could back out and we'd have a nice party.

I said the same thing to my daughter's fiancé at my daughter's wedding:

"It's not too late. You can back out, and we'll have a great party. But if you go through with this, I never want to hear about it again."

They're married over 25 years.

The tradition must work!

I'm still wondering if my son-in-law will pass this tradition on when his own girls get married.

They're getting older and the inevitable is coming!

MY FATHER'S RETIREMENT

My father worked until he turned 70. That night, he was going into work to retire. But when he got there, they told him that they had to lay him off.

He got a small payment from unemployment.

A few months later he got a Social Security check in the mail for $4,000.

That was a lot of money back then!

My dad didn't think he deserved it, so he sent it back. Honest to a fault.

The check came in the mail again, and he sent it back a second time, with his note explaining that the money wasn't for him.

They sent it back to him a third time, this time with *their* explanation:

You didn't retire at 65, so you earned this money by waiting. You are entitled to the money.

He finally cashed the check.

I know where I get my ethical behavior.

OUR WEDDING PICTURE

Our children were 3 years apart, about 10 and 7 years old. They were in our bedroom staring at our framed wedding picture on my wife's night table.

She was beautiful.
I was a skinny dork with black rimmed glasses, in a white tux jacket and black pants with a stripe down each side.

"What did you see in him, Mom?" they both asked.
"I thought he had potential."
She's still waiting.

HAND-ME-DOWNS

When my wife's nephew grew and grew, I used to joke with him that I would give him my old coats.

I told him they were hand-me-downs.

Then he got taller and taller. Eventually, he was just over six feet tall (I was only 5'9").
One day he came to a family affair and brought *me* a coat.
He called it a hand-me-*up*.

Now he gets his shirts from his second son, who grew even taller! His second son is 6'5"!

Another tradition continues!

DAD IN HOSPITAL

My father was in the hospital and not doing well. They gave him a little woolen hat to wear to keep warm, and he had difficulty eating. He was 85 years old at the time.

It was my parents' 48th wedding anniversary. Even though he wasn't doing well, we still wanted to celebrate such an achievement!

On their anniversary, we had a small party in his hospital room.

We brought a cake, fed him some of it (he was too weak to do it himself), and then we took the anniversary card out of the envelope and held it up so he could see it.

He was so weak. He could hardly talk. I had to read the card to him.

But then he summoned his strength and said,
"So where's the check?"

Caustic to the last.
I know where I get it.

The Diva

My mother was an opera singer. To do that job well, she had to have the personality of a diva. Which she did.

She was very proud, and she could really sing.

When my father was 83 and my mother was 82, they held a concert at their house. They let me invite a friend (and his wife) from work who was an opera buff. He and his wife both loved it.

I videotaped the event. My father played the piano. My mother sang with him accompanying her. Then my father played again.

What a treasure to have that video today.

My dad passed before my mother, many years ago. On Father's Day a few years later, while my mother was still alive, we thought it would be a good idea to see the videotape. We had the family to our house, and we all sat in our den and watched, while the tape began with my father playing the piano.

I had seen the videotape before. So I went out to the kitchen to get drinks for everyone, to make sure I could get back for when my mother sang. As I was getting the drinks, my mother walked into the kitchen.

"When am I on, already?" she asked.

Always a diva.

What about *me*?

It's a family in-joke now.

NEW ORLEANS

My wife took me to New Orleans for my 50th birthday. I had a cousin near there, and we made arrangements to meet her and her husband.

I had to bring something, of course, so what does someone from the Northeast bring to someone in the South? I thought of a box of TastyCake, a well-known Philadelphia product. Everyone likes TastyCake. I carried it on the plane.

When the driver of the shuttle to the hotel picked us up at the airport, I told him to be careful with the box of TastyCake. He said he would. Then he put it on top of our luggage, where it would be safe.

On his next pickup at the airport, the people got on the shuttle and the driver put their luggage in back. Right on top of our box of TastyCake!

Fortunately, the contents survived.

DINNER WITH THE IN-LAWS

We got along well with our son-in-law's parents. Sometimes we would all go out to dinner. Sometimes just the four of us, sometimes with the (married) children.

His mother and I had some similar traits. She would ask the maître d' for a table away from the kitchen, away from any draft, and of course, the table couldn't wobble.

My wife has learned over the years not to get offended when I demand the same things.

Away from the kitchen.

Not under a vent.

And most certainly, the table cannot wobble.

It was obvious why I didn't want a table that wobbled, or one situated under a vent. I couldn't remember why I wanted a table away from the kitchen. Then I found out.

Recently on a Sunday night we were at a restaurant with friends for a late dinner. The four of us were seated near but not too close to the kitchen. We weren't seated under a vent and the table didn't wobble.

The meal was very enjoyable.

As we were finishing, we could all smell the disinfectant wafting from the kitchen, as they were cleaning up.

It triggered the memory of why we always asked for a table away from the kitchen.

THE CHECKBOOK

Our son graduated college several years after our daughter, and he went on to medical school. Several months after his medical school graduation, my wife called me at work, late in the day.

"When you get home, you have to look at the checkbook. I must have made a horrible mistake."

"What's the matter with the checkbook?"

"There's too much money in it. Something's wrong."

It was a good thing I had only a short time left at work that day. Her comment made me so anxious that I couldn't wait to get home to see the problem with the checkbook.

As soon as I got home, I went through my wife's entries. Then I checked her math.

It was all correct.

"How can there be so much money in the checkbook?" she asked.

"We're not paying tuition anymore."

We had some spendable cash!

My wife took care of that in short order.

COOKED VEGETABLES

My mother used to serve vegetables that were cooked to death. We used to joke that all the nutrients were in the water she threw out. Maybe it wasn't that much of a joke.

My wife had learned how to cook *after* we got married. That's when I found out about blanching the vegetables and locking in the flavor and nutrients.

When we were married thirty years, we had my mother and sister over for a holiday dinner, with several other family members. When my wife served the crisp vegetables, my sister whispered loud enough that everyone could hear,

"Don't eat the asparagus. It's not cooked."

THANKSGIVING DINNER

When our second granddaughter was born, our daughter was home on maternity leave for several months, through Thanksgiving.

Our daughter wanted to have Thanksgiving dinner at her house.

She served a bread cornucopia, mashed potatoes and turkey (including the gravy).

I kept saying how delicious everything was, and where did you buy this stuff. Our daughter answered that she made it all from scratch.

Then came the pumpkin pie. Also delicious.

I again asked where she got it, and again she said that she made it from scratch.

She made *everything* from scratch.

Imagine how much time that took.

I finally told my daughter, "If you can make all this stuff from scratch, you have too much time on your hands. Go back to work."

AMNESIA

Many years ago, my wife hurt her ankle. The doctor put my wife's ankle in a cast immediately. No weight bearing at all.

She couldn't get to the washer/dryer to wash our clothes, and she couldn't run the dishwasher.

I had to learn how to run all three of those machines.

After 5 months in the cast, the doctor removed it and put her foot in a boot. For 5 more months!

So for a total of 10 months, I continued to run the 3 machines.

We'd heard terrible stories about people who didn't have a good medical outcome. We were so worried.

Then the boot came off, and my wife was told to walk on her leg to check it out.

It turned out that she was cured!

She went back to walking, with full weight bearing.

She was so lucky!

My wife was so happy that she immediately did a load of clothes and ran the dishwasher.

And I promptly forgot how to run the machines.

My friend told me that this is called Marital Amnesia.

My mother had no stupid children.

VISITING THE ANCESTORS

Several years ago, my wife and I took a drive to see her grandparents' row house in the old neighborhood. My wife remembered the address.

The street was so narrow that I had to drive slowly to avoid hitting the sidewalk.

We had to park on the sidewalk. Then we got out of the car and knocked on the door. No one was home. We got back into our car and slowly drove down the block.

At the end of the block, we saw some older neighbors sitting on aluminum folding chairs. They were suspiciously checking out the intruders as we drove down their block.

To allay their fears, I stopped the car and said to this one older woman, "My wife's grandparents lived near the other end of this block. We were just looking at their house."

"Who was her grandmother?" the woman said.

My wife told her their last name.

"I knew her," the lady said.

We smiled. "How did you know her?"

"When I was looking to move onto this block 53 years ago, I was down here looking at one of the homes, and this lady walked up to me and said, 'If you want to see the nicest house on the block, come see my house.' That was your grandmother."

53 years earlier!

FEEDING TIME

My wife's sister had her first grandchild by her son and his wife. A boy.

We flew west to attend his first birthday party.

The boy could *eat*! I picked him up, and at one year old, he weighed 26 pounds! Eventually, I had to give him back to his father. I couldn't hold him anymore.

Whenever the boy saw food, he simply ate it.

After the birthday party, we returned home to the east coast. Then her sister texted my wife about something the boy said.

A few days after the birthday party, his parents took him to the supermarket in his stroller.

When the boy saw all the food, he yelled,

"Snack!"

THE POT

We've been married over 50 years. During that time, my wife has had a pot in which she makes sweet and sour meatballs for the holidays. The granddaughters are always asking her to make them.

The other day my wife was out, and I was unloading the dishwasher. I noticed that her pot's lid was still missing the knob. The knob had been missing for over twenty years! My wife has to insert the tines of a fork into the little hole to remove the lid when it gets hot.

So I decided to finally get her another knob and surprise her. It wasn't a big thing. Right?

I had some time, so I took the pot and lid to the store. The guy in the hardware aisle said he'd take me to where the knobs are. There was another sales person at that location, and she told me that we had to determine the right kind of knob for the lid.

Suddenly this wasn't so simple.

The knob couldn't be metal, since it would get hot. It couldn't be plastic, since it would melt. She suggested a wooden knob.

She pulled out a small plastic bag with just the right size knob, but the 2 screws that came with the knob were too long (1.5", 1"). They were lengths for using the knob on a drawer.

So on we went to the screw department. The process was getting even more complicated!

The guy there said we had to determine the right length for the screw (which was 0.5"), as well as the right material (again?). We couldn't use either zinc or brass. It had to be stainless steel, so it wouldn't rust and contaminate the food. But he couldn't find an individual 0.5" stainless steel screw, so I had to buy an entire box of 100! (It was only $2.00.)

I told him that I wanted it assembled before I took it home and had to come back again. So this guy used a Philips screw driver and assembled the knob to the lid. It was tight as could be.

I took the finished product home and left the pot and lid on the kitchen counter, where my wife was sure to see it.

I got in bed, waiting for her to come home from her outing.

When she came in the door, she went straight to the kitchen. Then I heard uproarious laughter!

When my wife came in the bedroom, she was still laughing hysterically.

"That is so *sweet!*" she exclaimed. "But why did you get a knob *now*, after all these years?"

"I wanted to surprise you."

"I'm surprised the salespeople at the store didn't ask you why you just didn't buy me another pot."

"Before they could, I told them that the essence of the meatballs had been baked into the pot's metal material over all those years. The lid had to be fixed."

Then I told my wife about how we had to determine just the right material for the knob, and after that, just the right material and length for the screw. What a process! Took me over an hour!

My wife is still laughing.

APPENDICITIS

In college, I was friendly with another student, and in our second year we were on a sports team. We also played chess together. He lived in a nearby suburb.

One day I was visiting my friend in the suburbs and playing chess, when the phone rang. It was my mother calling for me.

I picked up the phone. "Hi, Mom. Is everything all right?"

My mother said, "Don't get excited, but your girlfriend is in the hospital."

"What's wrong?"

"She had appendicitis, and they removed her appendix."

"Is she all right?"

"Yes. Now get home quick, but don't drive fast."

It had been snowing, so I had to be careful as I was driving home on the expressway. The first curve heading toward home was a notoriously bad one, and as I rounded the curve, there was an accident in front of me. Cars were sliding in the snow, and I saw them running into each other.

7 cars in all, rear-ending in a pile-up.

I pumped my brakes, and my car came to rest about 5 feet from the last car in the pile-up. I was the 8th car in the 7-car pile-up.

I lucked out.

CATEGORY 3

WORKING

THE MEASUREMENTS

When I graduated college and started working, my wife and I moved into an apartment. Since my degree was in engineering, I did my own measurements for our bedroom furniture. I measured right up to the heating vents on the floor, to make sure the furniture would fit in.

Then we had to get carpeting. The man said they would send someone out to make measurements, but I volunteered to give them the ones I already had.

Easy, right?

When they came to install the carpeting, it went right up to the floor vents, but not to the walls. There was a 1.5" gap all around. The carpet installers were ingenious. They figured out how to correct the problem, by sewing a 1.5" strip of carpet to the main piece. Most of this strip would be either under the bed or along the back wall, so it was no issue.

Then the installer asked me,

"You made these measurements?"

"Yes."

"What do you do for a living?" he asked.

"I'm not going to tell you," I said.

FIVE KIDS

When I started working, I sat next to another engineer. He was Swedish, with blond hair. He was also a little on the heavy side.

Good engineer.

He and I would talk every so often.

One day I asked him about his family. He said he had five kids.

"*Five* kids!" I exclaimed.

"Don't worry. We figured out what's causing it now," he joked.

Several weeks later, the blond engineer came into the office and proudly announced that his wife was pregnant!

I immediately joked with him that I thought they had figured out the cause.

He said, "I guess we didn't have it nailed down as well as we thought. Back to the drawing board."

MY FRIEND THE DOCTOR

My friend left the company's PhD program, quit the company, and went to medical school.

What a different kind of choice.

After medical school graduation, his wife had a party for him. Several of his friends, including us, were there.

I was an avid tennis player back then, and I was having some pain in my right arm after a particularly hard night on the courts. So why not get some help from my friend, the new doctor!

I remember saying to him, "Now that you're a doctor, maybe you can help. When I lift my right arm and go like this, it hurts."

He said, "Don't go like that."

(Old line, but he actually said that)

He was joking (I think).

THE YEARLY DINNER

The PhD program had yearly dinners, and I was on the PhD program for a long time, since I did it while I worked. My wife and I attended a lot of those dinners.

Our first dinner was at a large well-known restaurant about a half hour from our plant. My wife and I left early to avoid traffic, and when we got there, several people had already arrived. The cocktail hour had begun.

We ordered drinks, but mild ones. Very little alcohol, so we wouldn't have any problems. Not at one of my big company dinners.

I got 2 whiskey sours for us, light on the whiskey. My wife drank hers, and then she asked for another. Same deal, light whiskey. Then she wanted a third.

I said, "Are you sure? After all, we don't drink."

"Yes, they're like lemonade. No problem."

I reluctantly got her the third drink, again with light alcohol. Down it went, rather quickly. "Don't go so fast," I warned.

"Ith's tho thmooth," she replied. Then she giggled.

I don't think I ever heard anything that ominous.

The final straw was when she said, "Tee hee. I can't feel my feet."

Nothing but coffee the rest of the evening.

Luckily, she was cool after that.

But I spent the rest of the night in fear.

SMOKING ON PLANES

Long ago there was smoking on airplanes.

I stopped smoking decades ago, so on a flight west I requested the non-smoking section.

They gave me the last row in non-smoking, with the smoking section behind me.

The guy behind me blew his smoke past me for the entire flight.

Even my hair smelled like smoke.

Eventually, all airlines went completely non-smoking.

But they didn't do it for the passengers.

Someone told me that the reason the airlines went completely non-smoking was that the smoke would get into the vents and stick to the vent walls. Over time and enough flights, the planes would become heavier and need more fuel.

It's always about money.

COLLECT CALLS

Well before there were cell phones, all long-distance calls cost money. At one point, my company stopped paying for safe arrival calls on business trips.

So when employees went on business trips, we all figured a way around this. We called home and asked for ourselves, collect. The employee could listen while the operator spoke. The spouse would say that the employee was not home, and would reject the charges. Then the employee would say thank you, and the spouse would hear the employee's voice. That way the spouse knew that the employee landed safely.

Everyone did that.

After my company stopped paying for the safe arrival calls, I flew to Cincinnati on business. As soon as I landed, I made the obligatory call, collect.

The operator had a strong Southern drawl, and she said, "Collect call from Covington, Kentucky. Do you accept the charges?"

That's right, Covington, Kentucky. It's right across the river, and that's where the airport for Cincinnati is. You rent a car and drive over the bridge.

I heard the operator clear as a bell, accent and all.

I expected to hear the usual refusal from my wife, but that's not what happened.

Instead, I heard, "Ankara, Turkey? What's he doing in Turkey?" My wife accepted the charges.

She insists that it was the accent.

PLOTTING BEFORE LAPTOPS

When I started working, I did all my work by myself. A few years later, my boss gave me a new hire right out of school to train. A stretch assignment for me, my boss told me.

I had help!

I gave the new hire a piece of graph paper and asked him to make a plot of experimental data that we got from a test. We didn't have computers to make plots back then, but we had engineers right out of school.

He brought the plot back to me, completed, and it looked right. Unfortunately, it had a brown circular coffee stain on it, and a dollop of mayonnaise.

I handed it back to him with another piece of graph paper.

"Please do it again, and this time don't include your lunch."

BEATING A LIVE HORSE

A few years after I started working, there was a system problem that involved a picture. The picture was of a single horse pulling a carriage through a large mud hole.

The question below the picture was, "How would you improve system performance?"

The answer was to add more horses to the carriage, making it easier for all of them.

Students who looked at this problem said that the company management approach was to add more whips. The phrase "more whips" came up often after we all saw that problem.

THE JACKIE MASON SHOW

Many years ago, someone told me about a show Jackie Mason was doing. When he came out on stage, he said that he didn't have any material. Instead, he asked the audience to name a topic, and he'd tell a story on that topic. He did it every show, for 4 weeks!

At that time, I was driving 4 other people to work to get money for gas, and it worked out for everyone.

On one ride into work, I mentioned the Jackie Mason show and what he was doing.

One of my riders said, "Remy, you could do that."

"That's ridiculous," I replied. "I'm no Jackie Mason."

"Sure you can," they all echoed.

My riders knew I was a jokester, but really. Jackie Mason?

So that night, on the way home, they insisted on me trying to do the Jackie Mason thing, right there in the car.

They mentioned a topic. I told a story.

This went on for almost an hour, when I dropped off the last rider.

I had done it!

But I was totally exhausted! Never again!

I had much more respect for Jackie Mason after that.

TRIP TO GERMANY

I went to Germany on business. Due to the time difference and the airline schedules, I went a day early to make sure I would arrive at the meeting on time.

In Germany the next morning, I went to my meeting. It went well, and the leaders of the German company took our team out to dinner at a very nice German restaurant.

I asked what was the specialty of the house? The waiter said it was "leber knoodle." The second word was pronounced with the 'K': k-noodle.

It sounded like something to do with 'liver,' so I ordered it.

The specialty came in a soup bowl, with about half an inch of light broth. The leber knoodle was in the center of the bowl. It was a gray (no kidding) ball of liver.

I tasted it. It was vile.

I ordered something else for dinner.

After the dinner, my colleagues took me to a German beer house, against my objections. I don't drink beer. Actually, I don't drink anything at all.

Nothing could stop them. Not in Germany!

They bought me a dark beer, in a very tall stein. It was at least a quart!

I tasted it. It was worse than the leber knoodle.
I couldn't drink any of it.
My colleagues finished it. They said that they would never waste a drop of beer!

THE DIVISION MANAGER

About ten years after I started working, I took an assignment in an analysis group. I had one of four metal desks in an area comfortable for 4 employees.

I went to a long meeting and returned to my desk. I opened the center drawer, and the central metal compartment for pens and pencils was filled with cold coffee.

What a mess! Pens and pencils *floating*!

"Who the hell spilled coffee inside my desk?" I yelled.

I knew it wasn't mine, since I didn't drink coffee.

One of the other engineers in my area said, "The Division Manager was just standing at your desk."

The Division Manager! 4 management levels up.

I had no idea why he would be at my desk.

"Oh," I said. "Then I'll just clean this up."

I tried, but I never did find out why the Division Manager was at my desk.

MY REVIEW

When I first worked in the analysis group, I'd learned that the way to get ahead was to take on more and more analysis jobs and get them done accurately, on time, and on budget.

After a year in this new group, I was asked to fill out my first self-appraisal. The appraisal cover sheet showed 5 categories, ranging from 1 to 5, with a box for each. You simply placed an "X" in the appropriate box. The rest of the form was for substantiation.

The appraisal ratings were: 1-Fails; 2-Nearly Meets; 3-Meets; 4-Exceeds; 5-Outstanding.

I had juggled 9 jobs at one time, and I got them all done on time and on budget.

So how to grade myself?

As a gag, I added Category 6: Super.

Of course, I placed the X in that box.

My manager didn't think that was funny.

No sense of humor.

When I was nearing the end of my career, we still had to do a self-appraisal. My boss at the time always wanted me to fill out the block in the appraisal form for Future Development Plans.

One time I put in a single word: **Retirement**.

He didn't think that was funny either.

ANOTHER YEARLY DINNER

After eight years I was still on the PhD program, and another dinner was held at the same large well-known restaurant.

My wife and I got there early again since we knew where it was, and when we walked in there was only one person there: the Division Manager. I introduced my wife to him, and he was rather pleasant.

Then he asked my wife, "How do you like the PhD program?"

My wife has never had trouble speaking her mind, and without any hesitation, she said to my boss's boss's boss's boss,

"I like the program very much. But why don't you give your PhD candidates enough financial support to get finished?"

I could never say anything like that to the Division Manager, so throughout the years I fought the bureaucracy for funding.

"I'll look into it," he assured her.

And he did.

Within weeks, I received sufficient funding to finish the computer runs associated with my dissertation.

I now send my wife to negotiate the tough ones.

THE TOKYO SUBWAY

A long time ago I went to Tokyo, Japan, on business.

It was brutally hot. I wasn't wearing an undershirt.

I was at the train station to take the train to my stop where the presentations were to be made. I heard the train arriving.

I was told by my boss (who was very tall) "If you're taking a subway in Tokyo, when you hear a train coming, lots of people will get off. Get behind a pole and let the hoards go by."

When I heard the train coming, I got behind a pole as my boss said. Hundreds of Japanese men came around the corner, having just gotten off a train. They all appeared to be around 5'4" with black hair, and each was wearing a white shirt, thin black tie, black pants, black shoes and black socks.

The hoard looked like a sea of lemmings all running toward the edge of a cliff.

I felt so tall. I was 5'9", almost a foot shorter than my boss. I could only imagine how *he* felt.

Once the hoard passed by, I walked to the subway train to board it. That's when I found out about the "pushers."

Pushers are people who jam riders inside the doors to make sure everyone gets on the train.

We were squashed in like sardines.

We could use "pushers" in some of our US subway stations.

THE PHD DEFENSE

I worked on my PhD for eleven years. Finally, at the end of my tenth year, I asked my thesis advisor, "When will I be done?"

He said, "Why don't you write up what you have now? Maybe it's enough."

It turned out to be enough, after all.

It was a good thing I asked.

I went to my thesis defense in May. It was scheduled for 10:00 AM on Tuesday. My wife went with me, even though she had 103°F temperature. She wasn't missing this event after all that time.

We walked into my college building, and we were early. The secretary told me that my thesis defense was scheduled in Room 311.

We went to the third floor and into Room 311. No one was there. The chairs were in disarray, and I had to straighten them out.

I went back down to the secretary.

"Where is my thesis committee?"

"The chairman of your thesis committee is in the basement running an experiment. I'll remind him."

We went back to Room 311 and waited.

About 15 minutes later, in walked an unshaven man carrying a folder. He was wearing a flannel shirt, jeans, and cowboy boots.

"Who is *that*?" my wife whispered.

"That's the chairman of my committee."

The other members of my committee sauntered in, including my thesis advisor. It was 10:15 AM.

I had my slides ready on the projector. My chairman asked, "How long will this take?"

"45 minutes," I answered.

"Keep it to a half hour," he replied.

I knew he was running an experiment.

Just then the senior engineering class came in to listen to my presentation. After I finished, they were excused, and the committee began the questioning.

One committee member said, "You solved the wrong problem." I almost fainted.

But I never had to say a word. The comment led to an intense debate with my thesis adviser, who defended the topic he gave me. When he finished, the issue had been resolved.

I was so relieved. My wife looked pale.

Then my chairman asked only 1 question. "How much computer money would you need to do something like this again?"

I replied with an amount.

Then my wife and I were excused.

We waited anxiously in the hallway. After 15 minutes, my chairman came out of Room 311 and saw us standing there.

He said, "The next time you present your defense, … oh, never mind! You passed!"

But it was too late. My wife had 2 coronaries in between his comments.

The last true autonomy.

THE COMPANY NEWSLETTER

I got my PhD while working overtime and supporting my family.

After I graduated with the PhD, the fellow who ran the company newsletter came to see me. He wanted to interview me about my dissertation.

I consented. Good company visibility.

Right?

I spoke with him for over an hour, and he took pictures of me for his article.

I told him the complex name of my dissertation, and he took copious notes. Lots of details about all the work I did.

When the newsletter came out, there was an entire page in there about me.

The only problem was that the title of the article read,

"It took Jay Porter 11 years to get his PhD."

That's what he got from all the discussion?

I still have a copy of the newsletter.

MANAGEMENT AXIOMS

Many years ago, one of my co-workers told me his 2 rules of management. He swore that our managers all lived by them:

First:
Whenever you feel like working, lie down until the urge passes.

Second:
When the going gets tough, find someone else to blame it on.

Did you ever have managers like that?

MONITORED PERFORMANCE

When I became a manager, an engineer was assigned to my group for his fourth 6-month assignment on a 2-year rotating program. The only problem was that for this assignment he was an engineer assigned outside his field.

I gave him simple assignments to start, but he had no idea how to proceed (of course not). He sat motionless instead of doing any work. I asked several senior engineers in my group to mentor him, but nothing helped.

I went to my boss and told him about this. He suggested "monitored performance," where you give an employee a specific task with specific measurements and document the performance (or lack thereof).

I said, "That won't work, since he doesn't have *any* performance."

When it was time for the engineer's review, he came to my office and I closed the door. The reviews ranged from 1 (fails) to 5 (outstanding).

I told him, "I'm giving you a 1 because we have nothing lower. I can't appraise your work, since you haven't done any work since you've been here."

He agreed. (Yes, he did!)

He had received 4's for his previous reviews, and my boss said to go to HR and ask how his previous managers could give him such good reviews.

When I spoke to the HR rep, he told me that his previous manager was on monitored performance.

THE GIRLFRIEND

One of the guys in my group had a year-end party at his house. My wife and I were also invited.

When we arrived, I introduced my wife to several of my employees. Then I introduced her to one of the engineers who was there with a lady. He said the lady was his girlfriend.

She wasn't wearing either an engagement ring or a wedding ring, so I knew that he hadn't popped the question yet.

We made some small talk, and then to be nice, I casually asked, "How long have you two been going together?"

He replied, "Twelve years."

"Twelve *years!*" I exclaimed in amazement. It came out before I realized it.

My wife and I looked at each other, then back at them. The engineer understood that we were having a difficult time processing what he had just said. So he added,

"Well, you don't want to rush into these things."

THE INTERVIEW

When I was the manager of the analysis group, we needed someone with nonlinear analysis capabilities.

An engineer submitted an impressive resume. We invited him in, and I interviewed him for an advanced position with nonlinear analysis.

He was from another country, and English wasn't his first language. It was difficult for him to communicate, and I was having trouble understanding him.

Our products required a team effort, and you had to be able to communicate with the rest of the team. It was my assessment that he would have had difficulty doing that.

I had to recommend him as a no-hire. I would have the HR group inform him later.

After about a half-hour of interview, I escorted the prospective engineer back to the lobby. During the entire walk to the lobby, his rubber-soled shoes squished on our hallway tile floors.

Loud sounds.

SQUISH, SQUISH, SQUISH!

They echoed in our hallways.

Then he said something (heavy accent) I could finally understand.

"I sorry for my shoes."

ONE SMART FELLOW

My company bought another company, and my division was combined with their similar division.

That's when I met a Fellow of the other company. He was very smart. It seemed like he could expound on any subject. Even though I already had my PhD, I was in awe.

One day, I said to him, "It seems like you know everything."
He replied, "Nah, no one could know everything. But I have a brother, and between us we have it covered."

OUR 25TH ANNIVERSARY

By our 25th wedding anniversary, I had given up management and was assigned as an engineer to a special project in another building. The project manager told me that I had to go to a company out west to present my work during a week in June.

"I can't," I replied. "My 25th wedding anniversary is in the middle of that week, and I want to stay married."

He kept arguing with me, and finally I said, "I'll go if you can figure out how to pay for my wife. I think I can sell it if I make it into a vacation for our anniversary."

The project manager figured it out, and I took my wife on a vacation out west during which I made my presentation.

My wife and I boarded the plane on the east coast, and we had an aisle seat and the adjacent middle seat. Seats were reserved well in advance.

We made ourselves comfortable, getting ready for the long flight west, when we smelled this horrible scent. We saw a guy heading for us, and it was his body odor!

He took the window seat next to my wife.

I called the stewardess over. It's our 25th anniversary. He smells! This is unacceptable.

She said they only had 2 seats left, both middles in different locations. So we had to sit there.

My wife leaned against me, and when the plane took off, the air conditioning kicked in. The smell abated somewhat, and we sat in those seats for the rest of the long flight.

We had to stand every so often to flex our muscles so we wouldn't get stiff. It also helped to get away from the smell for a few moments.

As we were getting off the plane, the same stewardess was at the doorway. She took her hands from behind her back and presented me with a large magnum of champagne.

"Sorry," she mouthed. "But Happy Anniversary!"

"Thank you," we both said, even though we didn't drink.

We decided to bring the magnum back with us. We were going on vacation to Florida with 3 other couples on the following Saturday, and we would share it with them.

My wife enjoyed the hotel pool while I worked on the day of our anniversary. I was with her for the rest of the vacation.

After a week of vacation, I put the magnum of champagne in the lower pouch of our garment bag before we left the hotel, planning to transfer it to a suitcase at the airport.

But I forgot.

We boarded the plane and took our seats. Then we smelled the same bad smell, and we looked up. The same third-world guy was heading our way! But thankfully, he took a seat a few rows in front of us.

When we were getting our baggage from the carousel in our home airport, there came the garment bag with the magnum hanging out of the lower pouch.

It was intact!

Our friends enjoyed the champagne at the airport on the following Saturday, waiting for our flight.

THE TECHNICAL TEAM

I worked with a fellow who had had senior positions before I met him, and he knew all kinds of details about designing our product.

He acted like a condescending big brother, but he taught me a lot. I used that knowledge during the rest of my career.

We were assigned to be a 2-man technical team, stationed in the local plant. Then we moved to a building that housed an entire major program.

My colleague got very friendly with the Program Manager's administrator, trading off-color jokes with her quite often.

We'd had many training sessions on sexual harassment, and I mentioned to him that I thought he was getting too familiar with the administrator. "I think you're giving yourself a large exposure. What if you say something one day that she doesn't like, and she reports you to HR? Then you'll have a lifetime of misery."

He dismissed my comment, waving his hands.

The next day he came into my office.

"I thought about what you said on my way home last night, and I think you're right."

To fix the problem, he never spoke to the secretary again.

A rather drastic approach, but it worked!

THE REVIEW CONFLICT

My colleague and I were scheduled to review one program, and we were designated as reviewers for another program's System Design Review (SDR).

For the first program, we were scheduled to provide our review results to the customer at their Pre-Ship Review (PSR). The review showed that there were red issues (unfinished paperwork), but they had a senior electrical engineer working on the final closures and they should be done in 2 days, prior to the PSR.

The SDR was scheduled 2 weeks later. No schedule problem. However, the SDR schedule was moved up, and the dates conflicted with the other program's PSR. The SDR was to be held in one facility, while the PSR was to be held 9 miles away.

We were both ordered by our boss to sit in on the SDR, since we were given seats at the front table with nametags, and our absence would be very visible.

We couldn't attend the PSR.

Instead, the Program Manager (PM) for the PSR gave our review charts to one of his engineers to present, even though we hadn't discussed the charts with him. The engineer presented our charts and gave the customer the impression that the program had major red problems (not our position).

The PM for the PSR called our boss, screaming, "Get those guys back over here to fix this!"

We were called out of the SDR, and we made the decision that I would present updated charts, while my colleague stayed at the SDR.

I talked with the senior electrical engineer who already closed most of the paperwork, as we expected. I updated our charts to reflect the improvement.

Then I explained our situation to him, and I said, "Sorry this happened. We had no choice."

He said, "I don't care what you say, I will *never* forgive you!"

I presented our updated charts and smoothed over the problem with the PSR customer. Then I drove back to the SDR and told my colleague what happened.

Still acting like my big brother, he said, "I'll take care of it with the senior electrical engineer."

Later we drove to the building where the PSR was being held, and we walked into the senior electrical engineer's office. My colleague explained the same situation I did, using almost the same words. Then the senior electrical engineer told him, "I don't care what you say, I will *never* forgive you!"

I smiled.

So much for the big brother routine.

I mentioned this event to the senior electrical engineer's A-level manager, who was at least three levels above him. When I told her what her senior electrical engineer had said, she replied,

"You mean the Doberman?"

AIRLINE PEEVES

When I received an assignment on a new program, I had to travel many times on business, including trips to the west coast.

When I knew of a trip well in advance, I booked my flights early to avoid the back of the plane. But many of these trips came up at the last minute. By the time I booked a ticket, I had to sit in the back of the plane. When I was seated back there, the airlines always did the same thing.

The stewardesses would roll the food cart (yes, the airlines served food back then) from the back galley past my seat, and I could smell the goodies. Then they took the cart all the way to the front and began their service.

By the time the cart got back to me, they were always out of my selection.

After a while I began to think they did it to annoy me.
This was one of my many airline peeves.

CUSTOMER HUMOR

Late in my career I was hired onto a program to evaluate the product for defects. I added another senior engineer and together we developed a review plan that would fit within the available funds.

To begin executing the plan, we embarked on a series of technical reviews for the program. We reviewed each of the subsystems of the payload to make sure the technical leads hadn't overlooked anything. We also had a technical expert in that field sitting in on each review, as well as the customer's Quality Manager.

After going through the subsystem reviews, the Quality Manager said that he was amazed that the reviews were so thorough.

I gave him my boss's name. "Why don't you tell my boss how satisfied you are?"

I'm still waiting.

During those reviews, we took a tour through the manufacturing bay, where we had a production line arranged for putting the products together.

That's when the customer's Quality Manager said, "I look at all the components that go into these products, and I remember that they're all provided by the lowest bidder."

I always say the same thing about airplanes.

SATURDAY MEETINGS

At one point on our project, we were struggling to make hardware deliveries on time. So my boss's boss decided to have 9:00 AM meetings on Saturday mornings for extra oversight.

I told him that I couldn't make it at 9 o'clock on Saturday because I exercised at that time. How about 11:00?

He said no.

I repeated my request.

He argued with me.

A lot.

Finally, I explained, "I take an exercise class from 9:00 to 10:00 on Saturday mornings. There are twenty-four 20-year-old hardbody girls in the class, and me."

He said, "I'll see you at 11 o'clock."

THE FRENCH DINNER

Our payload lead and I had to go to Paris, France, for a technical meeting with a French company. We were trying to get them to provide their hardware to our payloads.

We went with a Vice President and a Business Manager, our management contingent.

Our presentation and ensuing discussions were so well received that the management contingent took the two of us engineers out to dinner to celebrate, at a high-end French restaurant.

There were many courses, with a cart brought to the table for each one.

The bread cart.

The cheese cart.

The wine cart. Management bought 2 bottles of very fine wine, and they drank them, since both of us engineers didn't drink.

Then came the carts for the main meal. Vegetables, meats, and so on.

Then the dessert carts. French pastries, cakes, chocolates, etc.

16 carts in all!

But it was all delicious. Spectacularly so.

At the end of the evening, the bill came for the four of us. It was in francs, but after the conversion, it was still a lot of money!

I would rather have had a check.

FLIGHT TO FLORIDA

I was on my way to witness another payload installation. In all, I had been there as a witness 7 times.

The flight was non-eventful.

Then the plane landed with a loud jolting thud! Then another thud!

It was probably the hardest landing I'd ever experienced.

Over the loudspeaker the pilot said, "Take *that*, Florida!"

Can't do that today!

THE ROAST OF MY MENTOR

It finally came time for my mentor to retire. Since he was the MC for the retirement roasts for many years, they needed someone to do *his* retirement roast.

They trolled for a replacement MC, and no one wanted the job. No one could do as well as he did!

After asking 14 other people, they finally got around to asking me. I said, sure, I'd do it. I figured if I failed, they would say, 'No one could do as well as he did.' And if I succeeded, I could have a new career as a stand-up comedian.

When my company bought another company across the river, they sent my mentor as an ambassador to their plant. That's when he is known to have uttered his famous phrase, "I noticed that when you come here, you have to pass water."

Later, my mentor told me the same Alzheimer's jokes 3 days in a row. The bad thing was that I laughed each time.

He is also quoted as saying, "Marriage is not a perfect union. It's more like a sentence."

My mentor and I were on a business trip to Asia, and the plane stopped in Anchorage, Alaska to refuel. They ushered us into the souvenir shop, and there we saw a polar bear in a glass case.

The sign said that when shot, the polar bear was 9'4" tall and weighed 1,200 lb!

My mentor looked at the polar bear and said, "This would make a great Program Manager."

When we came back from Asia, we went through Hawaii. On the Japan Airlines plane to Honolulu, my mentor said to me, "I love the stewardess's accent, mixing up the l's and r's." Just then, she came over the loudspeaker system and said, "The prane will be randing in Honoruru shortry."

My mentor repeated that to me for many years. And after he passed, his wife did too.

My mentor told me the story of Becky and Morris, who were dating for a while. Becky called Morris on the phone. He answered, and she said, "I'll be over tonight wearing a slinky dress and no underwear. Be ready."

Morris replied, "So who's this?"

My mentor was an engineering A-level manager, and he knew how to get everyone's attention. At an off-sight meeting of the A-levels, my mentor's turn was scheduled after my A-level, Dr. W. My mentor stood up and said, "It's my honor to follow Dr. W and his very interesting speech."

Then he yawned.

There are so many more stories associated with my mentor, but these are the few I can still remember.

THE SPREADSHEET

I'm good with numbers. Always have been. At work I was both fast and accurate. I learned early that you have to double check your numbers, and I built checking into all of my spreadsheets.

As I became more senior, I was training younger engineers and showing them how to check.

One engineer brought a spreadsheet into my office and I did my usual spot check. I found errors immediately.

"Go back and fix these. From now on double check your work before you bring it to me. Put the double checks into your spreadsheet, and that'll make it easier for you."

Next time I checked his work, I found more errors.

Never worked with that guy again.

I didn't have time to be a quality control guy.

THE 75-YEAR-OLD MAN

Long ago, in a very busy Urologist's office, a 75-year-old man (it's not so funny, now that *I'm* over 75!) came in and walked to the desk.

The first lady behind the desk handed him a clear plastic vial with a twist-off top, and said, "Before anything else, we need a specimen."

He took the vial and walked down the hall to the men's room.

The office was very busy, and the staff lost track of the 75-year-old man.

After about 45 minutes, he appeared back at the desk with the vial and a big smile on his face.

The lady behind the desk looked at the contents of the vial, and she said, "We meant a *urine* specimen!"

PM'S RETIREMENT

Our Program Manager (PM), my boss's boss, was scheduled to retire.

We scheduled his roast during a program review, so the customer could attend. 144 people attended, with 14 speakers. It lasted 3 hours after dinner.

One of the speakers was the lead engineer from the customer's technical arm for the program. He came into my office during the day and asked for items he planned to use during the roast that night.

His speech went something like this.

"The Program Manager and I have known each other for years. We thought long and hard about what to get for the Program Manager of this project. Since the payload is based on a glass crystal, we searched the world to find one of the original 6 glass crystals that were used to develop the first payload. The glass crystals are is priceless, but we have one of the six."

The lead engineer stepped out from behind the podium with a box. He took a step toward the PM, who was sitting in front with his family at the guest of honor table. The lead engineer extended the box, and he *dropped* it! The box hit the floor, and everyone could hear the sound of glass breaking. The intake of air was so loud that it filled the room. Everyone stopped for several seconds.

The audience saw the lead engineer smiling, and people realized it was a gag. Everyone laughed.

When the lead engineer stopped into my office earlier that day, he requested any glass items we had discarded in the lab. That's what was in the box.

RETURNING FROM THE 9/11 TRIP

Everyone alive at the time knows exactly where they were on 9/11 (September 11, 2001). I was on the west coast with my entire team for a big presentation to the customer. We were trying to get them to change the contractor to *us* for the follow-on program.

We arrived at our facility on Sunday, September 9, to set everything up. We began our 2-day presentation on Monday, September 10, 2001. At the end of the day the customer thanked us but did not want to change contractors. They wouldn't be back.

We set up for the remaining portion of the presentation on Tuesday, but we didn't have much hope that many customers would return.

I woke up on Tuesday, September 11, 2001 and went down to the lobby of the hotel just before 7:00 AM. My project engineers were gathered around the lobby TV watching planes flying into the twin towers. On the east coast, it was almost 10:00 AM. The event had occurred over an hour earlier. They played the planes crashing into the twin towers over and over. Once the devastation started, no planes could take off, but those in the air could land. No one knew what would happen next. A very scary time.

We drove from the hotel to our facility on the top floor of our building, across the street from the airport. The entire customer contingent showed up. They had no choice. Their offices were at the airport, which was closed until further notice.

I introduced each speaker, and when a plane flew over, I stopped talking. Only after we realized that each plane was landing at the airport, did I continue.

We finished our presentation, but still the customer wasn't willing to change contractors.

We couldn't return home that night, since the planes for our reserved flights were grounded. We had to wait for planes to be allowed to fly again.

By Thursday, planes were still grounded. So my boss and our major subcontractor contracted a bus to take us across the US back to the east coast.

There were 2 drivers, and by law they could drive only 8 hours each. One was white, and the other appeared to be Mexican. As the bus was leaving the hotel, I used my cell phone to call my wife.

"We booked a bus. I'll be home in 4 days."

"Be careful," she said.

I jokingly tell people that she actually said,

"Are you really leaving?"

"Yes, we're on the bus."

"Well, don't. I checked your insurances and they're paid up. Wait for the next plane."

The second overnight stop was in Sterling, CO. I can tell you first-hand that it wasn't very sterling. There was a fly swatter in the sleazy motel room.

The next stop was South Bend, Indiana. We traveled through Nebraska and Iowa, and 900 miles of corn. One of our company guys on the bus was an expert on corn. He kept pointing out that the various fields were white corn, feed corn, yellow corn, etc.

When I got home, I told my wife not to serve corn with dinner. Not for a long time.

When the bus arrived at our plant on the east coast, one guy on our team who had been riding up front told us that what we'd thought was a Mexican driver actually turned out to be an Afghani!

RETIREMENT MC

Many years ago I was MC for our west coast rep's retirement dinner.

One of our program managers, who retired 6 months earlier, was coming out of retirement to attend. He sent me an e-mail that gave me my opening story.

The e-mail read, "I just opened my computer after 6 months of retirement, so I'm sending this e-mail as a test. If you don't get this, please let me know."

Everyone in the audience knew him, and after I read his e-mail, they ribbed him mercilessly after the retirement roast was over.

Here is a quip from the retirement dinner.

Our west coast rep was retiring, but he originally came from Texas. So I asked him, "Did you have a big place in Texas?"

He replied, "Yes. If I drove diagonally across my property, it would take me 2 days to get to the other side."

I said, "Yeah, I had a car like that once."

Again, old stuff but funny.

THE LAUNCH

I took my wife to Florida to see the launch of a rocket with our payload. We made a vacation out of it.

There were some issues during the launch window (12:00-12:15 each day), so they had to postpone for several days.

On the last day of our vacation, we didn't go to the launch site. We had to catch a plane at 3:00 PM.

But we could see the rocket from the local pier. We had lunch at a restaurant on the pier before going to the airport. We finished lunch and were standing against the railing when 12:00 arrived. It was a beautiful blue day.

A father and son (about 10 years old) were standing on the pier outside the restaurant waiting for the launch to commence. The loudspeaker announced a hold due to a parameter out of range.

The father said to his son, "Let's go. They're not going to launch today, again."

Then they left.

My wife asked if we should go too. We had to get to the airport, and it was at least a 45-minute ride.

"Let's wait the 15 minutes until the window expires. Then we'll go."

The rocket launched at 12:14. We saw it all. Taking off, heading down range, condensation trail. All clear as a bell.

The father and son missed it.

THE CHALLENGES

On my last program, my boss gave the team one of several challenges: He said something that we should all follow:

"It's better to shoot high and fail than to shoot low and get there!"

My boss also said a few other things:

"The organization is going to stay the same until it changes."

He defined The Rule of Holes: "When you're in a hole, stop digging!"

My boss negotiated the toughest concepts with upper management. But sometimes, things changed after he had an agreement. He called that, "Executive Amnesia."

Even though my boss said some things over the years that were pretty funny, he also had a soft side. I heard him say many times,

"We've got to win this. People's jobs are at stake."

One co-worker summed up my boss's work on the program with a quote from Samuel Johnson:

"Exert your talents and distinguish yourself, and don't think of retiring from the world until the world will be sorry you retire."

We all thought that my boss got there.

THE COLORADO LANDSCAPE

I went to a Colorado facility on company business with a Vice President. We landed at the Denver airport and since the VP was a large man, he chose to drive to the Colorado facility in a big Cadillac sedan (okay for a VP) rather than take a small plane and squeeze into those seats.

The VP drove down the main highway to our destination (about an hour and a half ride total).

On the highway he asked me, "How do you like Colorado?"

I looked around. It was like a moonscape. Brown ground and rocks everywhere you looked.

I said, "I'm from the east coast, and I like green and grass."

"There's plenty of green here," he said.

Just then, tumbleweed rolled across the road.

Yes, actual *tumbleweed*!

He never said another word about how green it was in Colorado.

THE OFFICE LOCATION

I worked for the same boss for 17 years. During that time, I was moved to different work locations in buildings within the same plant complex.

When I was working in an adjacent building, someone asked me, "How do you like working in another building away from management?"

I replied, "On the one hand there are plusses, and on the other hand, there are advantages."

Another time, I was asked the same question. This time, I replied, "There are plusses and minuses. I'm still waiting for the minuses."

THE LASER POINTER

We held a major review with our customer for our program's follow-on contract. We hadn't won the follow-on yet.

I prepared to give the overall presentation for our design, where I showed pictures. I described how all the subsystems came together to provide the functions required by the customer.

I took a back-up laser pointer, in case there was any difficulty with the primary one. The laser pointer has to have the proper color based on a certain wavelength of light so that it can be seen on the metallic screen.

I double checked prior to the presentation, and both pointers were the right wavelength. It was easy to see where I was pointing. Everything was a go.

As I started, the primary laser pointer stopped working!

I smiled, since I was *prepared*.

I put the primary laser pointer away and took out my back-up laser pointer. As I pointed it at the screen, the bottom screw-in cap fell out, and so did the batteries!

Amidst the roar of laughter, I bent down, picked up the batteries, slid them into the pointer, picked up the screw-in cap and tightened it (which I obviously had not done previously).

My colleagues managed to remind me about the laser pointer batteries, right up to the day I retired.

THE DESIGN REVIEWS

I worked with an engineer who was the Design Review Manager in charge of all program design reviews. He'd been doing this job for decades, and he had checklists in every area, developed over an entire career.

I learned a lot from him.

He was about six feet tall with thinning gray hair and a wide infectious smile.

Design reviews are loaded with pressure. Each engineer has to think of everything in his area. The customers are very sharp, and they'll skin you alive if you don't know your stuff.

And it was the Design Review Manager's job to make sure each design review ran smoothly. He had to know a lot about everything, and he grilled the presenters mercilessly at preparation reviews, prior to the customer event.

We never let that smile fool us.

He was tough!

Someone joked to me, "I don't envy his job. Look at him. He's only 27."

ONE BAD DAY

My company moved everyone to a different facility many miles away. My Vice President was turning 55 (the youngest age at which an employee could retire).

He said to me, "J.L., I'm turning 55, and I'll be one bad day away from retirement."

I replied, "I think you'll find that once you can retire, those bad days won't seem so bad anymore."

I knew from experience that my statement was true. And as it panned out, the VP lasted another 9 years.

Other employees have said the same thing to me over the last segment of my career, and I gave them the same response.

They've all told me that I was correct.

LONG-TERM EMPLOYEE

Years ago, a new employee came into our division, and I was given the assignment to mentor him. He was very sharp, and he quickly moved up through the ranks.

Decades later, he became an A-level manager, and my boss.

One of his tasks was to represent management by attending the Long-Term Employee (LTE) dinners.

At our next staff meeting, my boss mentioned that he had just attended that year's LTE dinner, and there was an employee getting recognized for 55 years of service. I knew him very well, since I worked with him for 20 years at that time.

That was when I had 44 years of service to the company.

My boss said to me, "J.L., are you trying to catch up to him?"

I replied, "Let me explain something to you. He hasn't retired yet. I'm 11 years behind him, and I'm not making any headway."

This long-term employee eventually retired with 57 years of service. I never did catch him.

THE HOTEL CHAIN

One year our company had one of its year-end parties at a large downtown hotel (part of a chain).

900 people were in attendance. There were employees and significant others from 2 different divisions.

The hotel's ballroom was large enough to accommodate all of us.

On my program, we had an on-site representative at one of our vendors. This representative spent 3 years at a hotel (part of the same chain) near that company.

He was at the next table at the year-end party.

There were door prizes at the party.

He won one of the door prizes.

It was a free night at one of their hotels.

He was laughing the hardest.

A FELLOW

Near the end of my career, I worked for my company over 40 years at the time. My boss, a Vice President, asked me, "Would you like me to put you in to become a Fellow?"

I gave him a one-word answer.

"Now?"

I was retirement age!

You had to fill out 27 pages for the application. I said, "No. Too much work on the application."

"Let me know if you change your mind," my VP said.

I went home and told my wife.

"You should do it. I'd be so proud," she said.

I went back to work the next day and ran into my friend, a Fellow for many years.

When I told him the VP's offer, he said, "You should do it. You should have been a Fellow a long time ago."

"Too much work on the application." I said.

"I can help you fill it out," he said. "Besides, you get more money."

"I'll do it," I said.

I was selected to be a Fellow, and I remained a Fellow until I retired.

THE OVERALL PRESENTATION

We won the next generation version of our program many years ago. On the program, one of my tasks was to review all charts to be presented at major design reviews (3 days of charts). I would look for and remove any inconsistencies. If I didn't don't do it, the customers would be certain to find them.

Five years into the program, we were preparing for a scheduled major design review. I proofread the entire set of charts (~400), finding inconsistencies and fixing them. During the review, I gave the overview presentation to provide the overall design. I'd been doing that presentation for the last 6 years, as the design continued to evolve.

This time one of the customers came up to me and said, "I always love your presentations. That's when I usually find out how it all comes together."
"Tell my boss so he can put it in my review."
I gave him my boss's name.

I'm still waiting.

THE PROVERB

There is an old proverb: "If it ain't broke, don't fix it."

Many years ago, we had several other ways of putting it at work.

1. Our CEO said, "If it ain't broke, fix it *anyway.*" The CEO wanted the technology improvements.
2. I said, "If it ain't broke, don't *break* it."
3. The deputy program manager said, "If it ain't broke, I can fix *that!*"
4. The payload lead said, "If it ain't broke, it doesn't have enough *features!*"

LONG-TERM MARRIAGE

We've been married over fifty years. Definitely a long-term marriage. Someone once asked us, "How do you stay married for such a long time?"

There are several answers I heard over the years.

1. Yes, dear (This is a proverb. 'Anything you say' is a well-known addition)
2. We agreed early on that I would make the big decisions and she would make the little decisions. I'm still waiting for a big decision to make.
3. We realized early on that we should take stress out of our lives. Instead of waiting for the weekend, we go out to dinner to destress twice during the week. I go Tuesday, she goes Thursday (vaudeville comedian).
4. Separate activities. She has her things, we have our things together, I have my things. That way we get some space. It's like our money. She has her money, we have our money, that's it!
5. Separate bathrooms (this is a requirement once you get older)
6. Low expectations

I believe Item 6 is the best. Here is the proof.

We were on a cruise and saw a funny comedian. He spotted us and asked my wife, "You two married?"

"Yes."

"How long have you been married?"

She replied, "50 years."

Then he said, "Can you share some wisdom on how you were able to do that?"

Without missing a beat, my wife said, "Low expectations."

She brought the house down and stopped the comedian in his tracks.

Item 6, for sure!

<u>Divorce</u>:

My best reason marriages don't last:
Man thinks woman *won't* change;
Woman thinks man *will* change
Both are wrong!

LONGEVITY

Our division had been sold to another company, and the new company announced the closing of our plant. They were moving everyone to their own plant out west.

The 2nd in command at the new company made the announcement in the cafeteria in our plant. He read a written explanation of why the plant was closing. He was obviously told by the company lawyers not to deviate from the written text that was carefully crafted by the company legal department.

If anyone would have told me then that I would still be working in the same building more than 20 years later, I would have said they were crazy.

Yet, there I was, still working for the company all that time.

Nearing the end of my career, my colleagues and I had many retirement discussions. My colleagues always asked me how long I wanted to live.

My answer was always the same.

I wanted to live to be 140 years old.

They would ask, "Why in the world do you want to live so long?"

I answered the same way each time.

"I want to suck as many dollars as possible out of that pension plan!"

PENSION CALCULATIONS

My wife used to ask me why I kept all of my pay stubs throughout my entire career. They filled a cabinet and according to her, they were clutter.

After the plant closing was announced, I created a retirement spreadsheet in 3 days. I then refined this spreadsheet right up to the day I retired.

The company pension formula was well documented. The company's pension estimator reported three possibilities: 1) the full pension, 2) the 50% survivor option, and 3) the 100% survivor option. The 2 survivor options were reduced 13% and 25% respectively so the beneficiary would continue to receive the amount should I pass first.

I had formulas for each pension option built into my spreadsheet, to check company calculations.

Federal law says the company must pay you your full pension while you're working, once you turn 70½. I was still working at that age, and I began to receive the full pension.

After a few years, when it was time to retire, I had to submit a form requesting a calculation for my selected option. This would determine what my pension would be.

I selected the 100% survivor option and submitted the form. I knew what the amount should be. I had been checking it for a long time.

They sent me back a form letter stating my pension amount.

Unfortunately, they used the 50% survivor option.

No wonder I continued to check them.

I retired a few years ago at the end of January. I then received my first pension check on February 1st. It was the same amount I was getting for my full pension, before I selected the 100% survivor option. I thought this was strange, since I expected a 25% reduction.

I thought they knew what they were doing.

Incorrect!

Later that year, in September, I received a letter from the company pension department. They made a mistake in the February check. It should have been reduced by 25% for the 100% survivor option. In February, I expected the reduction, but by September I had completely forgotten that the February amount was for the full pension.

They had overpaid me, and I had to return the money. To do this, they would be taking 1/3 of the error out of each of my pension checks for the last 3 months of the year, October, November and December.

My wife asked why I saved all my pay stubs. I answered her, "They're my record so I can prove my data, in case the company ever makes a mistake in my pension calculations."

Any questions?

100% SURVIVOR OPTION

As I mentioned, when I retired I selected the 100% survivor option for my pension payments, with the commensurate 25% reduction. It's like buying an insurance policy, where my wife would continue to collect my pension (the same amount) if I pass first.

However, the company pension has a standard kick-up feature.

That means that if my wife passes first, within the first 5 years of my retirement, my pension reverts to the full amount (no more 25% reduction).

I explained this to my wife in all its details, and she understood. Then I told her,

"So at 4 years and 364 days, watch out!"

THE EXECUTIVE PERK

Many years ago, I was given the opportunity to participate in a company executive perk. I was allowed to invest a portion of my salary, and the company would provide a guaranteed interest rate until I retired, with the rate continuing through my selected 20-year payout period. A no-brainer!

The first of the 20 payouts would occur on March 1 in the year after I retired. Even though my original company sold my division off, it turned out that my original company would still be providing the payouts for the executive perk.

As I said, I kept all of my pay stubs from the time I started working. You never know.

When I didn't receive the first planned payout on March 1 following the year I retired, I called the executive perk phone number of my first company.

I'd reached a live person over the years, but as a cost-cutting improvement, you could no longer speak to a live person. You had to leave an e-mail.

A lady called me back 6 days later. I inquired about the payout, and she looked me up by my social security number.

"You're on our records as an active employee of your company," she said.

"But I retired in January!"

"We'll have to research this," she said.

I always assumed that my second company would have given any necessary information to my old company, but that is clearly not the case.

This just proves again that I was smart to save all those pay stubs!

After many days, a lady from my old company called me to say that they finished their research, and everything had been straightened out. Since they had missed the March 1 date for the first payment, I would receive it as soon as possible, most likely the coming Friday (a month and a half late).

On that Friday I checked with my bank. A deposit had been made, and they told me the amount. I noted that the company did not make an adjustment for interest for the extra month and a half.

This proved the validity of my keeping all of the my employment details and the executive plan all these years.

FIRST RETIRED FLIGHT

In February, during the month after I retired, my wife and I were heading to Mexico for our first scheduled vacation (actually, it was only a trip, since I was on permanent vacation). The flight required two legs to get to the final destination.

Since I'm a frequent flyer, we happened to get kicked up to first class for the second leg of the flight.

I felt pretty good about retirement.

When we boarded the plane, we found 2 people sitting in our first-class seats. I looked at our tickets to verify that we were in the right place, and we were.

I said to the lady sitting in our aisle seat,

"Excuse me, I think you're in our seats."

She raised her head and almost scraped her nose against the overhead bin, replying,

"*We* are in Row 3!"

"*This* is Row 4!" I replied in kind. "You can tell by the sign above the seats," I said, pointing at the Row 4 label.

They moved to Row 3.

My wife said I was being rude.

A RETIRED PHONE CALL

I was retired for a while when the phone rang. It was my old boss. She had moved on to manage other programs.

We talked for a while, and then she asked me if I would be available to help out on one of her new projects.

I said, "It sounds too much like work."

I then told her that if she could deal with all the booked trips (as I said, we no longer take vacations) in my schedule, maybe we could figure something out.

I e-mailed her my trip schedule.

She e-mailed me back, saying that she couldn't find a way to accommodate my schedule.

That's the last I heard of it.

Note that I didn't say, "… if she could *work* with my schedule, maybe we could *work* something out."

That would definitely be too much like work!

CATEGORY 4

VACATIONS

ROAD SIGNS

We were in San Francisco on a vacation with the kids. They were younger, around 10 and 7.

We had seen lots of signs for roads named for prominent people, such as the Admiral Nimitz Highway.

As we were coming off the Bay Bridge, my wife said, "Look. They named the road after Menachem Begin, prime minister of Israel."

The sign read, "Begin Highway."

On the same San Francisco trip, we were driving with our kids seated in back.

We had a movie camera that required four AAA batteries. The batteries were at low charge and had to be replaced.

I had four extra batteries and I took them out and handed them to my wife.

We pulled over and I removed the low-charged batteries from my camera. I handed them to my wife, and she dropped all 8 batteries (new and old) in the same pile.

We drove to a store where I could buy new batteries.

The kids were still laughing 3 hours later.

THE STEAK DINNER

In June of the same year, we drove to Niagara Falls on vacation with the kids.

On Saturday night we went to the Top of the Falls Restaurant, the only restaurant that overlooked Niagara Falls. The restaurant rotated 360 degrees, giving the patrons a spectacular view.

It was our anniversary. Everything was special.

I ordered a steak to celebrate.

The waitress said, "We're out of steaks."

It was Saturday night at 7:30! The busiest time of the week!

I was so mad that I said, "Then I guess I can have the 3-lb lobster for the same price."

"I'll check," the waitress said, and she left.

She returned a few minutes later. "We found you a steak, sir."

I smiled at my wife and she smiled back.

I ordered the steak rare. The steak arrived and it was overcooked. I told the waitress, and she took it away and brought me a rare steak, cooked the way I ordered it.

We thought it was funny that they were able to find a second steak for me right away.

We never sent anything back before that night. We've been making sure we get what we ordered ever since.

DUNGENESS CRABS

We're from the east coast. We eat Maryland blue point crabs. A dozen jumbo blue points just about does it for both of us.

On our 25th anniversary vacation, my wife and I took a trip to San Francisco's Fisherman's Wharf. The street vendors were selling small paper cups of crab meat for a dollar. I got one.

The crab meat was good.

I asked my wife if she wanted to go inside and have lunch. I could do crabs on the west coast. She agreed.

The vendor said, "You can order here and eat inside. What would you like?"

Still thinking like an east coast-er, I said, "A dozen crabs, please."

"These are *Dungeness* crabs," the vendor said. "Have you ever had them?"

"No."

"Maybe you should start with *one*," he said.

"Okay," I replied, listening to him.

We went inside and they brought out one Dungeness crab. It weighed about 2 lb!

One was plenty!

BOURBON STREET

My wife took me to New Orleans for my 50th birthday. Our trip started on Halloween eve. It was like being at a mini Mardi Gras. The city was ablaze with this holiday weekend.

The first person we saw, when we left our hotel for a walk at around 5:00 PM, was a lady dressed as the Wicked Witch of the West. She was wearing all black with the high pointed hat.

Very cool so far for my birthday.

We were walking farther down on Bourbon Street when my wife heard music. We stopped to look into the open floor-to-ceiling windows of a bar.

She saw a handsome shirtless guy with a six-pack and long hair, dancing on the bar. Soon she was dancing on the sidewalk along with him.

He saw her and then he was pointing at her. Then she was pointing back at him.

Then he motioned for her to come inside. That's when she saw it. All guys.

It was a gay bar.

My wife was mortified.

We quickly moved on.

They were all laughing.

So was I.

A RESORT VACATION

Many years ago, we went to a resort on the east coast of Mexico. Puerto Aventuras. The resort was new and they had a great promotion. $700 for the week for both of us. It was all inclusive, and air fare was also included.

Our friends also took the promotion.

The other husband and I entered the tennis doubles tournament. As it turned out, we won. They gave us a certificate for being International Tennis Doubles Champions. (Rule #1)

Every morning a Mexican made me an omelet to order. Great omelets.

The Mexican was short. He was a Mayan.

At the end of the week I took out a $5 bill to tip the cook. That was a lot of money back then, but he was worth it.

A stranger ran over to me and said, "What are you doing?"

"What are you talking about?" I asked.

"You can't *do* that," he screamed.

"Do *what*?"

"Give him that big a tip. That's what he makes for the *week*! You'll ruin it for the rest of us!"

When the man left, I gave the cook the $5.

THE FRENCH RESTAURANT

Long ago we were going on a vacation to Paris. We'd heard about the attractions there all our lives, and we were so excited.

Before we left, we read the Sunday paper. The travel section said to try certain restaurants in Paris for real Parisian food at reasonable prices.

We took the page with us.

For an authentic dinner on our last night in Paris, we went to one of the restaurants suggested in the paper. The people there spoke only French.

We used to smoke when we were younger, but no longer. Not for a long time. And it was difficult for us to tolerate other smokers.

But the Europeans smoked a lot. When we entered the restaurant recommended in the newspaper, I asked for a table with no smoking, making myself understood with hand signals.

The host took us to a rectangular table for 6 and sat us against the wall, opposite each other. The other 4 seats were empty.

Then they brought 4 more people to our table. The restaurant was filling up.

I assumed these 4 people were also non-smokers. But that was *not* the case. Within 5 minutes they all lit cigarettes!

I went to the manager. "I asked for no smoking," I said, irritated.

In broken English, he replied, "Yes, those 2." He was pointing to the 2 seats at our end of the table.

ORIENT BEACH

We were on vacation in St. Martens in the Caribbean. It was beautiful. We were told to go to Orient Beach. A topless beach. Don't miss it.

We drove there, parked in a large lot, and walked onto Orient Beach. It was beautiful, as advertised. There were padded chaise lounge chairs with umbrellas fifty feet from the water. We got 2 chairs, and we happened to sit next to 4 young American girls on spring break, all in 2-piece bathing suits.

A beautiful blonde and her husband walked up to the seats on my other side. They sat down and she took off her cover-up. Then she simply removed her top!

She was well endowed.

She went topless and thought nothing of it.

Twenty minutes later, the American girls told my wife that the beach about half a mile down was all nude. A moment later we were walking in that direction.

Of course we were! Had to check it out!

Our first encounter was when we passed a well-tanned leathery 70-year-old man, completely nude. He was walking toward us.

That's when we learned that most who went nude, *shouldn't*!!

THE SODA MUG

We went with our daughter and her family on a vacation to Disney World. We had the adjacent room so we could monitor the kids when we babysat. Our kids had a 9-day stay, but we would leave after 4½ days and go to the beach for the rest of our vacation. I'd been to the beach there before, and I knew how to drive there.

Our son-in-law's parents lived on the other side of the state, and they planned to drive across the state and take our adjacent room for the remainder of the 9 days.

My wife and I got the soda package, since we don't drink. It cost $11, and the package came with a large mug like a beer stein. We kept filling it up for our entire stay.

Definitely worth the $11, since we both used it.

But to save his parents $11, we handed the mug to them as we were leaving (washed, of course).

We made the same family trip to Disney World for the next 3 years. Each time, our son-in-law's parents took our room for the second half of the stay. We got the soda package each time, and the stein became our communal soda mug. We even had a little ceremony for the handover to our son-in-law's parents.

We all talked about that mug for a long time.

THE OLYMPICS

One year we were on a Baltic Capitals cruise, and we docked in Tallinn, Estonia, the capital of the country. A group of us from the ship took an excursion, and we had an Estonian guide who showed us around.

We asked the guide if Estonia was friendly with Russia. The guide gave us a funny look, and then he told us the following story.

The Olympics were to be held in Moscow, and the Russian leader was to give the opening speech. A speech writer gave him a wonderful monologue, and then it was time.

The Russian leader stepped to the microphone and began, "Oo, oo, oo, oo ..."

The writer rushed to the podium and whispered, "Sir, not there! Please start on the next line. You're reading the Olympic logo."

Did we strike a nerve?

THE DESSERT BILL

We went on a trip to Europe with 20 other people. 11 Couples in all.

My birthday occurred just before the trip, and our traveling companions knew all about it. Once we checked into our hotel, we all went to a local restaurant. Dinner for 22! It wasn't easy to accommodate us, but the restaurant did it!

Dinner was very nice, and then the other 20 people bought me dessert for my birthday: a slice of pie. A very nice touch, I thought.

I gulped it down, since we had to run to an appointment back at the hotel. I got my portion of the check and paid, leaving the others to finish.

After the appointment, I happened to look at my receipt from the restaurant.

They put my dessert on my bill. It was $7.

When we saw the other 20 people the next day, I told them what happened.

They all laughed.

Even though the other people bought me the dessert for my birthday, not one of them thought to reimburse me.

Some of them still laugh about it. It comes up around the time of my birthday.

And they still don't offer to repay me.

SPRING BREAK

One year after our Disney World family vacation, we continued on to the beach. There we found a comedy club.

The comedian was rather raunchy but excellent, and then he went into a routine with audience participation.

He saw 4 college girls sitting 2 rows behind us.

"College?" he asked.

The girls nodded.

"Spring break?"

They nodded again.

"Which college?"

They answered together, "Morehead State."

As the audience laughter was dying down, he said, "I'm not goin' anywhere *near* that."

My wife is not a prude. She was laughing harder than anyone else.

THE NEWLYWED GAME

One year we were on a Caribbean cruise, and we submitted our names in a jar to enter "The Newlywed Game," 30-50 category. They selected contestants based on how many years they were married. They consisted of an older couple married 65 years (over 50 years category); we were married 45 years (30-50); the next couple 25 years (5-30); and the 4th couple one week (real newlyweds, 0-5).

Our daughter and her 2 daughters were in the audience of around 150 people. The girls were laughing at every answer.

The MC asked a question, "What nickname do you call your wife during playtime?"

It was the 25-year-married couple's turn, and the husband answered,

"Oh, I couldn't tell you *that!*"

The laughter got louder.

The MC continued, relentlessly.

"Oh, come on. You're among friends."

More uproarious laughter. Even the other contestants were laughing.

After several pushes and cajolements, the husband finally relented. He answered,

"Mommy!"

The audience went berserk, laughing hysterically for about 5 minutes.

Our 3 girls were leading the pack.

ORDERING LUNCH

We were at our resort in Mexico, and we were sitting on the beach. The waiter came to take our lunch order.

I ordered a cheeseburger with onion and tomato. I ordered in Spanish, practicing my language skills, as usual. The waiters all spoke both languages.

My wife ordered a plain hamburger, in English. No bread, no onion, no lettuce, no pickles, no cheese. No nothing, she said.

The waiter asked, "Plate okay?"

On our cruise through the Panama Canal, we were cruising past a port in Mexico. I went up to the outside grill on the upper deck at the back of the ship, to have lunch.

I ordered ahi tuna rare. I'd had it before, and it was delicious. I told the cook that I wanted nothing else. No bread, no fries, no onions, no cheese, no tomato.

He said, "Plate okay?"

Is it associated with Mexico?

ANYONE FROM THE SOUTH?

At the same resort in Mexico, we met a couple from a city in the south. The husband asked, 'Do you know anyone in my city?'

I answered, "Not now. But my cousins lived there 40 years ago."

We went to dinner with them, and since it was unusual for us to meet anyone from their southern city, that became the topic of conversation. My wife mentioned that my cousins lived in their city 40 years ago. She mentioned them by name, Sam and Marsha.

The husband's head snapped up and he looked surprised. He said, "Sam and Marsha? Sam and Marsha *who*?"

My wife told them their last name.

The husband said, "They lived next door to my mother!"

"Are you *sure*?" my wife asked.

"Did your cousin Marsha play a character named Green Riding Hood?" the husband asked me.

My cousin Marsha was an actress, and I remembered the character. Green tights and tunic that looked like Robin Hood. Fedora type hat, with a green feather in it.

When I composed myself, I said, "Yes, she did."

"Your cousin Marsha did that character for our daughter's 4th birthday party!"

40 years ago?
Really?

THE SAFE

For my 70th birthday, my wife took me to Hong Kong and Thailand. We went to 4 places. Hong Kong, Bangkok, Chang Mai, and Phuket. We went back to Hong Kong for the last night, so we could go to the Hong Kong airport and take the plane home. We packed up at the hotel, and we were ready to take the shuttle for the airport.

My wife had placed her cell phone in the safe, since it contained her pictures from the entire trip.

"Hon, I can't find my cell phone. Please look in the safe," she said.

I looked, but I didn't see it.

We have a thing about safes. We always do a final check to make sure we don't leave anything in there.

I felt all around on the felt-covered bottom. Nothing. I looked again. Still nothing.

We removed the felt bottom. Nothing.

We called the hotel and they came up. They looked in the safe too. Nothing.

My wife was distraught. All those pictures lost!

We called the porter, and after several minutes, he arrived with a cart.

"Let me look one more time," she said.

My wife felt around in the safe, and then she moved both hands out to the sides.

There was her phone!

It was standing against the left side. It was black. The safe was black. No wonder we couldn't see it!

She found her phone!

Disaster averted!

SLAYING OF THE FIRST BORN

We were back at the same resort in Mexico for another vacation. This time we brought another couple. We had the lockout for them, and the units had a connecting door. That was a common thing in Mexico.

It was an easy vacation. Plenty of room for everyone.

One day the four of us were sitting by the portion of the pool that was near the beach. It was about 3:30 in the afternoon.

It suddenly got dark, and then a low-lying dark gray fog started to creep in from the ocean. It slid over the beach and up toward the pool chairs. The fog was about 12" deep, and it covered our ankles.

It reminded us of the slaying of the first born in the movie *The Ten Commandments*.

"Thank G-d you have an older brother and I have an older sister," I said to my wife.

It was the eeriest thing any of us ever saw.

We still talk about it.

CRUISE SHIP STATEROOMS

Some cruise ships number the staterooms in consecutive order. We'd been on many cruises with staterooms numbered that way. Every time.

One year we took a cruise down the coast of Alaska. My wife took the elevator to Deck 8 and followed the sign to staterooms 8001-8097. She was looking for our stateroom, 8056, but couldn't find it.

She knocked on the door to 8055.

A guy answered the door.

"I seem to have lost my stateroom. It's 8056," she said.

The guy explained that some ships have the odd staterooms on one side and the even ones on the other side.

"Your stateroom is not lost," he said. "It's on the other side."

My wife was mortified.

And of course, she kept running into the guy from stateroom 8055 many times during the rest of the cruise.

Recently we took a Mississippi riverboat cruise. On that cruise, we learned where the term "stateroom" came from.

It turned out that the earlier riverboats had several cabins on board, and they named them after various states.

Hence, "state"-rooms. The name stuck.

ANOTHER NEWLYWED GAME

We were on a South American cruise with 18 other people. One of the couples put their name into a jar and was chosen to play "The Newlywed Game."

The women answered the questions first.

The MC asked our friend the wife the first question:

"What is the first thing your husband touches when he gets up in the morning?"

Our friend said, "My hand."

Everyone laughed.

After all of the questions were put to the women, they brought out the men.

The MC repeated the first question to our friend's husband. "What is the first thing you touch when you get up in the morning?"

The husband answered, "Gently, touch her, to wake her up."

"All right," the MC said, "and which part of her body do you touch?" The MC was pointing down his arms.

"Her shoulder," the husband said.

"And then where do you go?" the MC asked, waving his hands.

"To the bathroom."

The wife almost fell off her chair.

I took video on my cell phone.

We laugh every time we watch it.

THE DENTIST

During one stay at our Mexican resort, the resort gave out popsicles at 2:30 PM every day.

We arrived on a Friday, and on the Thursday almost 2 weeks into our 4-week stay, we were sitting by the pool when the staff came by with a cold cart full of popsicles.

We each got one, but they were small.

I removed the wrapper and as I was about to eat it, my wife said, "Don't bite into the popsicle."

Kiss of death!!

I bit down on it gently.

My front tooth crumbled and broke off at the gum line.

I was distraught. I asked the concierge to find me a dentist, hoping against hope that it could be fixed.

I got an emergency appointment that evening at 6:00 PM. The dental practice was in a strip mall near the supermarket, and we knew where it was. We arrived just before 6:00.

My wife looked at the dental practice to make sure they had the proper equipment. Then she commented on how modern the practice was. They had better equipment than my dentist back home! No wonder people get their dental work done in Mexico!

She gave them the green light. OK to proceed.

The lady dentist took one look and said that I needed an implant. Then she took x-rays and examined my tooth for infection. Luckily there was none.

I knew that implants took several months, and I wasn't going to be in Mexico that long. I needed something temporary. The lady dentist said she could build me a "flipper" to wear until the implant work could be performed.

I agreed right away.

She took impressions and I made another appointment for Saturday morning. The flipper would be in by then. In the meantime, I arranged for a flight home on Monday, and a Tuesday appointment at home with an implant specialist.

On Saturday morning, I arrived at the dentist's office, and she had the flipper waiting for me. She used a handheld tool to grind and adjust the flipper until it fit in my mouth properly. It took over half an hour for her to complete the process.

I got the bill from the dental office in Mexico. It was for the emergency appointment on Thursday evening, the examination, the x-rays, and the fitting of the flipper on Saturday morning. It was 2,100 pesos.

But when I converted it to dollars, the total was just over $103!

When I got home, I paid for the implant separately. I waited for it to grow into my bone, and then I had my general dentist take impressions and install a cap over the implant.

I won't mention the total price at home, but it was a lot more than what I paid in Mexico.

I understood why so many of the people we meet in Mexico have dental work done while they're there.

CELL PHONES

We were on a cruise to Vietnam and other far-east countries, and we booked a side trip to Angkor Wat in Cambodia.

Unfortunately, my wife got sick and couldn't go. I had to go by myself, overnight.

The bus driver for the tour in Cambodia kept telling us to remember our cell phones.

After the 4th time he said this, I asked him why he kept reminding us about our cell phones. He said he always did that. Then he told me the following story:

"I had a group a while back, and I was giving them the usual reminder about cell phones. There was a 14-year-old boy in the group, and I looked at him and jokingly asked him again, "Do you have your cell phone?""

He answered, "Of course. You've reminded me several times already."

He then proceeded to pull the cell phone from his pocket.

Except it wasn't a cell phone. It was the TV remote from his hotel room.

When I was in Thailand, I took a cell phone picture of one of the monks. They have nothing but the orange robe and sandals they wear.

Except for one item.

A cell phone.

AQUI

One year we were at our Mexican resort and I wasn't feeling well. I said to my wife, "Maybe I ought to see a doctor to find out if I have a stomach bug."

"Okay, let's go," she replied.

We walked to the free doctor associated with the local pharmacy. If you go to her, it is expected that you will purchase any prescribed medications from her pharmacy.

The lady doctor spoke perfect English.

After finishing her examination, she said, "I think you do have a stomach bug. I want to send you to the lab for a blood test and a stool sample, so I can prescribe the right medicine."

"Okay," I said. Sounded good to me.

"The lab is in the hospital."

I was apprehensive, but my wife and I packed into a cab and went to the hospital. It was about 5 miles down the same street.

The lab was on the 3rd floor. The woman behind the counter was in her late twenties, and she spoke just enough English to make sure the hospital got paid. After taking my insurance information and driver's license for ID, the woman handed me a clear plastic cup with a red twist-off top. It was obviously for the stool sample.

Then she said in broken English, "You can do this here or take it home with you and bring it back."

One of the Spanish words that I learned is the word for "here." It is "aqui" (pronounced "ah-key").

I said to the woman, "I'm not going home to do this." Then I tapped on the counter. "Aqui," I said.

The woman raised both arms and waved her hands across her body and back 3 times.

"No aqui! No aqui!"

When my wife and I stopped laughing, I said, "Aqui banio!" ('Banio' means 'bathroom,' the most important word I learned in Mexico.)

I never meant that I would give her a stool sample right there on the counter.

WHERE SAYINGS ORIGINATE

When I retired, we were on a trip on a riverboat, Amsterdam, Netherlands to Basil, Switzerland. It would be several hours until the next stop.

The cruise guide suggested that everyone go up on the top deck so we could enjoy the scenery.

Once we were seated on the top deck, the guide's voice came over the loudspeaker, annotating the castles and other items we were seeing.

When there was a lull in the attractions, to maintain continuity the guide explained where certain sayings originated.

She first told of the family structure in the old days, and how they washed. The father went first, then the mother, then the children, from the oldest to the youngest. If there was a baby, it went last. That's how the saying originated, **Don't throw the baby out with the bathwater.**

She then told of how people drank in olden times. Sometimes, the men would drink themselves into such a stupor that you couldn't tell whether or not they were dead. After a few days, they would bury the man.

To make sure he really was dead, they would tie a string around his finger, pull the string out of the coffin up through the ooil, and attach it to a bell. If the man woke up in the coffin, he would wiggle his finger and the bell would ring. That's how the saying originated, **Saved by the bell.**

It is *not* a boxing term.

CRUISE TRAVELERS

One year in October, we took an 18-day cruise from San Francisco through the Panama Canal, stopping in Havana, Cuba, and finishing in Miami.

Most travelers were older and retired, and they were available to take a cruise in October.

All cruises have a show each night. On the first night, the cruise director opened the show by saying, "Did you see the kids on this cruise?" There was a long pause, as everyone looked quizzically at each other.

Then he said, "They're in their early 50s. Brings the average age here down to 79!"

THE TOUR GUIDE

On the same Panama Canal cruise, we stopped in San Diego to avoid bad weather on the east coast. This meant that we had to skip a scheduled stop in Cabo San Lucas. The ship provided a bus tour through San Diego for the unscheduled stop, to replace the planned tour.

These are 3 quips from the San Diego tour guide.

The tour guide showed us the water park in San Diego. It was built during a water shortage.

Duh!

He showed us a sign on Route 5 (a federal highway):

Cruise Ships Use Airport Exits

He then said, "Ask me any question and I'll answer. If I don't know, I'll make something up. You'll never know anyway."

The tour guide was 87 years old at the time.

We wished we had guides like that all the time!

THE CPAs

On the same Panama Canal cruise, we picked the specialty restaurants for the sea days. We always take the option to share the table with others, since that's how we meet as many people as possible.

On our first sharing night, we met a couple from New York City. He was a retired CPA.

He gave us his definition of CPA:

Cleaning, Pressing and Alterations.

I met another retired CPA on the same cruise. His definition was:

Cutting, Pasting and Adding.

He claimed that's what they actually did long ago, BC (before computers).

Hadn't heard those before.

I'm not a CPA.

ICE ON A CRUISE

On one of our cruises, soft drinks were included. Prior to the start of that night's show, at the back of the show lounge they had soft drinks on the bar, with 3 small ice buckets. When I went to get our soft drinks, the ice buckets were empty, and there were no tongs in sight.

One of the show people was standing nearby, and I asked her if she could please call someone to get us ice and provide some tongs.

She did, and a waiter brought out a large bucket of ice and filled the 3 smaller ice buckets. Then he put out 1 pair of tongs.

There were 5 of us waiting for ice.

I asked him, "Can you bring more tongs?"

The waiter said, in broken English, "Use it one person at a time."

THE KEY CARD

On the Panama Canal cruise, due to the change in itinerary because of weather, we stopped in Costa Rica much later than planned. The ship replaced the original cruise-line-sponsored excursion with another one sponsored by the cruise line.

For any excursion, to get off the ship you have to show them your stateroom key card. You show it again to get back on. That way they can track who's back and who's not.

It was pouring in Costa Rica!

We showed our key cards to get off the ship, and we walked to the bus in the rain with our umbrellas. When we got on the bus, we put our wet umbrellas on top, and our bag and raincoats between our feet.

What a mess.

About a half hour out, my wife said,

"Where's my key card?"

You can't get back on the boat without it.

Talk about panic-stricken!

She looked through her coat pockets and then through her purse. Twice. No key card.

Exasperated, she said, "Stand up and we'll look for it!"

I stood up. There it was, on my seat. She had it in her hand when she got off the boat, and in the rain, she didn't have time to put it in her purse. She put it down on my seat so she could slide over.

"How did you not *feel* that?!" she exclaimed.

Of course, it was my fault.

THE COLOMBIAN GUIDE

On the Panama Canal Cruise, we stopped in Cartagena, Colombia. We took a tour that started at 8:00 AM, and the Spanish speaking guide spoke English very well, but he had a heavy accent.

After a long ride and a stop at a local museum, we got back on the bus. We had been on the tour for a while, and it was 10:30 AM.

The guide then gave out paper bags to all the passengers. He said, with his heavy accent, "This is a snack. It's a turkey sandwich and morphine."

??

"How bad could a turkey sandwich be to need morphine?" I said out loud to my wife.

The lady sitting next to me overheard my comment. She was from Puerto Rico. She obviously spoke Spanish as well as English, and she translated the last word.

"Not morphine," she said. "Muffin."

PHONE SERVICE

On one of our cruises, we signed up for a simple LTE phone package. This package was only to make emergency calls.

About halfway through the cruise, we received a text message from the phone service saying that they were shutting off our LTE service.

So if the phone service turns off your phone, how do you call them to get it turned back on?

It's just like looking for your glasses.

SUPERMARKET STORIES

On one of our cruises, we met a couple who lived on the west coast. When I mentioned that I was writing a book about Rule #1, she told us the following 3 stories to prove that the rule is universal:

#1) I went to the local supermarket and got my items. In the checkout lane, a disabled lady worked as a bagger. People were buying Easter baskets.

The bagger said to me with a pout, "I've never had an Easter basket."

I felt so bad that I bought her one.

The next time, the same bagger told me, "I forgot my lunch today, and I'm very hungry."

I said, "Would $5 buy you lunch?"

The bagger said, "$10 would be better."

I will never stand in that lady's checkout line again.

#2) I brought 6 of my own cloth bags to the supermarket. That way, the food could be separated to make the bags lighter so I could actually lift them!

When I checked out, I said to the bagger, "Please don't make the bags too heavy."

He filled 4 bags. Each one was very heavy. I could barely get them into the car.

Next time, I had the same bagger. I said, "I told you last time not to make the bags too heavy. This time could you spread the items into all 6 bags, please?"

He said, "Lady, you have to work harder."

#3) I went out for burger rolls. While I was at the supermarket, I figured I would also buy a dozen eggs.

I stood in a line with a man doing the bagging.

When he finished putting my two things in a bag, he said, "You want some help getting these out to the car?"

"No thank you."

"I'm off in a minute and going anyway."

"All right then."

He walked me out to my car. When we got there, he asked, "You don't mind loose eggs at the bottom of the bag, do you?"

Rule #1 is definitely universal.

This is *proof*!

CHILDREN

THE SPECIALIST

When we got married, we lived in my parents' house for a year until I graduated college. I got one job offer, and I accepted it. Then I started my first (and only) job with my company, and we moved to an apartment across the street from a hospital.

Our daughter was born while we lived there. When she was 9 months old, my wife was changing her. At that moment, our daughter jumped off the dressing table and hit the floor.

It was our new baby's first traumatic event.

My wife, almost hysterical, picked our daughter up, grabbed our check book, and ran across the street toward the hospital. She was waving our check book and yelling, "Get me a specialist!"

The problem was that I had been working only a few weeks. We had $11 in the checking account.

Our son was born almost 3 years later. By then my wife had it figured out, and nothing bothered her.

I always tell her that it's a good thing we never had a third child.

She would've lost it.

A 4-YEAR-OLD'S CONCERN

When our daughter was 4 years old, we had all four of our parents over for Father's Day. Both fathers were sitting on the sofa watching a baseball game, when our daughter came halfway down the stairs holding her crotch.

"I think I have a little blood," she said.

I don't think our fathers breathed for over an hour.

It turned'out that she was chafed and a little red.

THE NEIGHBORHOOD DELI

When our son was nearly 3 years old, I took him to the neighborhood deli for lunch.

We got a booth, and we ordered our sandwiches.

The waiter brought them, and we began to eat. When we were finishing, our son looked at the wall adjacent to the table, and saw a cockroach crawling up the wall.

"Daddy, what's that?" he asked, rather loudly, pointing to it.

Did everyone in the deli turn around to look at us? It certainly felt like they did. It was like the old commercial for the stockbroker E. F. Hutton.

The deli manager rushed over and told me, "Your sandwiches are on the house. Please go."

We left right away.

I never took our son to that same deli again.

THE PEDIATRICIAN

When our son was still nearly 3 years old, we took him to the pediatrician for his yearly checkup.

The doctor wore glasses, and he had black hair and a beard. He was very nice, and he took good care of our kids.

As part of the examination, the doctor had to remove our son's diaper. As soon as he had the front folds of the diaper moved to the side, our son sprayed the doctor's face.

I'll never forget seeing his beard dripping from our son's performance.

Later, the doctor told us that because of our son, whenever he did an examination of a male child, he always covered him with a separate diaper.

THE SWIM CLUB

When our children were small, we belonged to a swim club. That's where I taught them both how to swim. If I remember right, I threw my daughter in the deep end and told her to swim. I waited by the side of the pool in case she got in trouble.

My wife yelled at me for hours.

But our daughter became a water safety instructor, so I guess she really learned to swim!

One summer, our daughter was 5 years old and our son was 2. In fact, he was very quiet. He hardly ever said anything (boy, has that changed).

We were out at the swim club on a beautiful day, and we had seats around the pool. We asked the kids if they wanted anything from the snack bar. Our son was standing next to us, and he softly said,

"I want a popsicle."

We smiled, since he said something, but we didn't think he needed all that sugar.

My wife told him, "No, it's too much sugar."

Then our son put both arms straight down next to his sides and yelled at the top of his lungs,

"I WANT A *POPSICLE*!!!"

He screamed so loud that he turned red. It highlighted his blonde hair.

I got him a popsicle.

THE BIRDS AND BEES

When our daughter was 5, my wife saw her walking between our house and the one next door, holding hands with the 6-year-old boy from 2 doors down.

My wife called our daughter in for dinner. While we were eating, she asked our daughter, "Was that your boyfriend I saw you holding hands with?"

"Oh, *no!*" my daughter replied emphatically.

My wife served soup, and then she continued to needle our daughter. "Does your friend know about the birds and bees?"

We had taught our daughter about the birds and bees, using the proper language.

"Oh, yes. He knows all about them," our daughter said.

My wife almost spit her soup across the table. Then she composed herself long enough to ask, "*How* does he know about the birds and bees?"

"I *told* him!" our daughter said exuberantly.

My wife could barely *breathe*!

But to understand how bad the situation could get, my wife continued, "Just *what* did you tell him?"

"I told him that when a boy and girl want to have a baby, the boy inserts his penis into the girl's vagina, and 9 months later, out comes a baby, through the rectum."

Our daughter went on to become a doctor. She understands *all* the details now.

POTTY TRAINING

When a young boy was 3 years old, his parents were having a difficult time getting him potty trained.

It was so bad that he would go into a corner and do his thing in his diaper.

One day, his older sister decided she was going to get to the bottom (no pun intended) of it. She sat him on the potty and told him he had to do his business there.

Still he refused.

So she said to her little brother, "If you go on the potty, your doodies will flush to Florida, and we can see them when we go to Disney World."

He was potty trained a few minutes later.

THE SCALE AND THE AIR

When our son was 4 years old, it was time for his yearly checkup at the doctor.

Before we left for the doctor, my wife put our son on the bathroom scale to see how much he weighed.

He stepped on the scale, and then he looked up at her and said, "Mommy, how much do I cost?"

She was so stunned that she couldn't reply. But what she was thinking was, "A fortune!"

When our daughter was 8 and our son was 5, our daughter ran into our bedroom and yelled,

"Get him out of the den! He's breathing my *air*!"

THE GUINEA PIG

When our daughter was in second grade, the teacher was showing the class a long-haired female Peruvian guinea pig.

The teacher said that she would raffle it off and one lucky student could take the guinea pig home. The students just needed to get permission from their parents to enter the raffle.

So our daughter came home and asked for our permission.

"Sure," I said. "There are 25 students in the class. What are the odds?"

Out of 25 students, she won.

Of course.

She brought the guinea pig home. She named the guinea pig Mopsy.

But when it came time to give the guinea pig a bath, my wife was pressed into service. That's when my wife noticed a spot on Mopsy's bottom.

My wife put some cream on the spot, but after several days, there was no improvement.

We went to the animal store, and the proprietor said that this was a *male* guinea pig, not a female.

Cream was definitely not going to change *that*!

THINKING

When our son was 9 years old, he was talking to my wife.

"Mommy, are you thinking about what I'm thinking about?"

"I don't know," she replied. "What are you thinking about?"

"I'm thinking about *me*!"

Sounded just like my mother.

It runs in the family!

TV ANNOUNCER

When they were little, we took our kids to Disney World for the first time.

They loved it.

We spent a week there, walking all over the facility and seeing the many attractions.

Then we spotted one where you could become a TV announcer for a brief session and read a script in front of a TV camera.

The kids were too young to be selected, but they would have loved doing it.

So instead, they kept yelling at the Disney people to pick me! And pick me they did.

They gave me a jacket and tie to wear, and they sat me at a table in front of a set of bright lights and a TV camera. Then they told me to read the script on the teleprompter.

I could see my wife and kids watching as I became a TV announcer for a few minutes.

They all loved watching me do this. So much so, that I asked the Disney people for a copy of the videotape.

Their response really surprised me.

They could not provide it for me, even though I told them I would pay for it. They claimed it had something to do with copyright laws.

Really?

My wife and kids were disappointed, but not as much as I was.

THE PURSE

When we got to the Disney World resort, we went straight to one of their big attractions. The luggage was stored at the hotel. We'd get there later.

It was Typhoon Lagoon Water Park, a separate island in the Disney complex. We decided to walk around the island before taking any of the rides.

We were in Florida, and it was a gorgeous blue sky on a very warm day.

We stopped several times to take pictures. One time my wife put her purse down, and we took several pictures with the kids in different poses.

As we were walking around the rest of the island, my wife said, "I forgot my purse!"

We rushed back to the spot where she put it down, and it was gone.

The worst thing about it was that she had all our documents and cash in her purse. The tickets, the plane reservations home, etc. We hadn't gotten to the hotel room yet to put those items in the safe.

We ran to the entrance to ask if anyone had returned her purse, and there was a couple there, handing her purse to the attendant.

"That's my *purse!*" my wife screamed from a distance.

The attendant made her identify the contents, and then they gave her the purse.

Everything was inside. The couple had found the purse, and was turning it in, intact.

We offered the couple a reward, but they declined.

Of course. No reward needed in Disney World!

MY 40TH BIRTHDAY PARTY

When I turned 40, my wife threw a party. She invited my boss (6'8") and his boss (6'4") to my party.

My son was a young teenager. He saw my 2 bosses standing in my kitchen door talking to me. They were so tall that they darkened the room.

My son walked over, looked at both of them and then at me. Then he said, "Daddy, are you standing in a hole?"

BEDROOM DOOR CLOSED

When our son was 18 and home from college, he knocked and then opened the door to our bedroom. He walked inside our dark room while we were having a discussion about a topic we didn't want him to hear.

We stopped talking to each other right away.

We spoke with him in the dark bedroom for a few moments, with light only from the hallway.

I don't remember what the topic was, but it was *very* important to him.

Then he left and closed the bedroom door. The room became completely dark again.

We resumed our discussion, and after about 30 seconds we heard him giggle.

He was on our side of the door, listening in the dark.

He never left.

My wife wanted to kill him.
I laughed for about a half hour.

DAUGHTER'S SORORITY

Our daughter was in the 6-year medical program: 2 years at college, 4 years in medical school.

During her college stay she joined a sorority, Sigma Delta Tau (or SDT).

She affectionately said it stood for "Spend Daddy's Trillions." I said, you mean, "Spend Daddy's Thousands."

They had a special sorority event, and the parents were all invited to attend.

Many of her sorority sisters had split families, where the parents had gotten divorced. It became a little cumbersome for her sorority sisters to introduce their various contingents that came to these events.

So our daughter found a way to simplify her own process. When she introduced us to her sorority sisters, she said:

"These are my biological parents."

DAUGHTER'S FIANCÉ

In the third year of her 6-year medical program, our daughter entered medical school.

On the 3rd day in medical school, she called my wife.

"Mom, I saw this guy in my class. He is so handsome. If he's not married or engaged, he's mine."

"What if he has a girlfriend?" my wife asked.

"Fair game," she replied.

They're married over 25 years now.

He always says he never saw her coming.
Smart man.

RURAL ROTATION

When our daughter was in medical school, her third year was a clinical year, and they had rotations in the hospital.

Her first rotation was at her own hospital in the Emergency Room (ER).

For her second rotation she was to be sent to a rural hospital, again working in the ER.

I asked her, "Why don't they let you stay at your own hospital for your second ER rotation?"

"Well, at my city hospital I get to treat knife wounds and gunshots. At the rural hospital, I'll get to treat cow bites."

THE SCIENCE OLYMPIAD

The Science Olympiad is a science competition among the nation's high schools.

Our son was on his high school's Science Olympiad team. When he was in 11th grade, the team was 7th in the country. Toward the end of 12th grade, our son had become the captain of the team of 8 seniors and 8 juniors.

In that year's Science Olympiad, thousands of students were competing from high schools in 30 states. In the finals, only the 2 state winners participated. 60 schools in all.

The final event was held at a local state college, close enough that we could drive there. We were surprised that only one other parent was there, and the three of us sat together behind our team.

We arrived at the Olympiad at the end of the event, and we found out that our son had taken a 2nd, a 4th and a 5th in his three events. It turned out that the teams each got points for 1st thru 10th place, and he earned 9, 7 and 6 points for his team, a total of 22.

Then we listened as the judges called out the top ten teams, from 10th place to the winner.

Irmo, a magnet school from California, and Gompers Secondary School also from California, had each won the event several times in previous years. In this year's competition, these two schools had split the 1st place results in the individual events.

Our team had no 1st place wins in any event. Just a lot of other top ten placements.

They announced the 10th place team. Then the 9th place team. When they got to the 8th place team, the judge announced the other team from our state!

I heard my son say to his teammate, "Did we come in 11th?" After all, they had no 1st places.

7th thru 4th went by as we listened carefully.

Then 3rd place went to Gompers.

And 2nd place went to Irmo.

Our team was completely dejected.

Then the judges announced the winner.

It was our son's high school team.

The kids were all was screaming and cheering.

The three of us parents got treated to the thrill of a lifetime.

Our son's team had won a national championship!

It turned out that our school had won just enough points to get by the two magnet schools.

You certainly couldn't make *that* up!

MEDICAL RESIDENCY

Our daughter was a medical resident in NY City. While there, she did a rotation at a nearby major cancer center.

She called me to tell me the following:

"A woman presented to the ER (Emergency Room) with severe abdominal pain. I diagnosed her and then rushed her to the OR (Operating Room). The woman had an ectopic pregnancy (embryo in the Fallopian tubes), and if it ruptured, the woman would become septic and probably die. I made the correct diagnosis. I literally saved the woman's life."

"You've told me stories like that before. What's different?" I asked.

"That was two weeks ago. Today I had a patient at the cancer center, an older man. My attending told me, 'We're losing him. Call the family in.' I told them at the nursing station, and they made the call.

"We worked on the patient for several hours and pulled him through. My attending told me to go practice giving good news.

"I found the family in the waiting room. Among them was the same young woman I saved in the ER two weeks earlier. Then I found out that our patient was the father of the young woman who I saved two weeks earlier!

"I told all of them the good news.

"Then the young woman said to me, 'Someone sent you to our family!'"

COLD IN BOSTON

After medical school and residency, our son-in-law got a fellowship in Boston. Since they were married, our daughter had to find a local position so she could go with him. She was hired to open a practice in an area south of Boston.

For the grand opening of her new practice, 4 of us (her parents and his parents) all drove there for the big event.

It was February in Boston. 12°F outside.

We were staying near our daughter's practice, and after the event we decided to drive into Boston to see our son-in-law's office.

The wives were in the back, I was driving, and our son-in-law's father was in the passenger seat up front. He was wearing earmuffs. We, the fathers, were both freezing.

His mother said from the back seat, "Turn down the heat! We're boiling back here!"

Really?

We turned down the heat, and the fathers were freezing even more. But it wasn't enough.

His mother yelled from the back, "Open the window, or my clothes are coming off!"

We cracked a back window.

Then we texted ahead. Our son-in-law had hot chocolate waiting for us.

I can still feel the cold.

MEDICAL SCHOOL DATING

Our son was in medical school and dating a pretty classmate who happened to be Chinese. Her parents were both doctors, and they had a beach house at the shore.

The young lady invited our son to the beach house for the weekend, with her family.

When they got to the place, her entire family was there. There were approximately twenty of them, including aunts, uncles and cousins.

My son joked with her cousins, and then the 14-year old cousin suggested volleyball on the beach.

They started to go outside when her mother said, "Where are you all going?"

The 14-year old cousin couldn't remember our son's name, so he said, "Goin' out on the beach to play volleyball with, uh, ... the white boy."

The mother was mortified.

My son still laughs about it.

THE UNUSUAL CASE

When our son landed a position in his radiology practice, one of his first cases took place when he was on call, literally all by himself.

A 50-year-old lady presented at the ER with severe abdominal pain. She'd tried to conceive many times but was never successful.

Her physician requested an ultrasound study, which was done at my son's practice.

When our son reviewed the files, there seemed to be 2 masses, one on either side of the lower abdomen. He also noted that the woman didn't have a uterus.

In his report, he wrote that the masses were possibly undescended testicles, and that the woman could actually be a man, even though she had been living as a woman for her entire life!

The next day, he consulted with others in the practice, and they agreed with him. He submitted his report as it was written.

This condition rarely happens, but it was a correct call.
It certainly was an unusual case!

GOLF

My son has two boys. Between work and the two boys, he doesn't have much time for recreation. He has to force the time to play several different sports.

One day he called me to say that he rolled his ankle and tore something.

"What were you playing?" I asked.

"Golf."

I said, "Golf? I didn't realize that you *played* golf. Also, I never heard of anyone getting hurt playing golf."

"It's worse than that," he continued. "It was *miniature* golf."

It turned out that he stepped on one of the curbs that keep the miniature golf balls in play, and he rolled his ankle over it.

He may never hear the end of that.

INTERNATIONAL TRAVEL

Our daughter was in Denmark on business in the summer of 2016, before the presidential election. It was just after the Republican debates.

The election was coming.

Donald Trump vs Hillary Clinton.

Our daughter took a cab to the airport to go home.

The cab driver asked, "You American?"

"Yes."

"You have about 350 million people?"

"About."

"And you had to pick *those 2* to run for president?"

FRIENDS

OLYMPUS WHEEL

We met our friends when I started working. The husband worked in my group, and we carpooled.

We remained friends for many years.

He left our company and went to work for an investment company in Manhattan. They had to move a good distance away to minimize his commute.

One time we were visiting them at their new house, and the wife told us a story about her father.

He was from the old country, and he learned to speak English when he came over to the USA, but with a heavy accent.

At dinner one night, he asked his daughter for "Olympus wheel."

Our friends were both baffled. No matter how hard they tried, they couldn't figure out what her father was talking about.

It turned out that it was due to his accent.
He was asking for "a lean piece of veal."

She talked about this well after her father passed away.
She still talks about this.

GHETTO CHILDREN

Many years ago, we held a summer tournament at my athletic club. My friend came from New York to play in the tournament. For his job, he was an English teacher, teaching summer school English to ghetto children in Manhattan.

When he got there, he sat down, took out papers, and started grading them.

After a while, I saw him shaking his head, and I asked what was wrong. He showed me one of the papers. The assignment was to write a composition about your father.

"Read the opening sentence," he said.

He handed me one of the papers.

The title read, "My Father."

I read the opening sentence. It said,

"I used to go to sleep at night dreaming that I would wake up with enough strength to strangle the son of a bitch to death."

It was many years ago, but I remember that opening sentence clearly.

It was obvious that ghetto children live in a totally different world.

THE BAG LADY

One summer many years ago, I was playing gin at my swim club with some of the guys.

The following story was told to me by one of the players, my friend, a retired detective from the city police department.

The police picked up a guy on a Wednesday for selling drugs. The guy was already a 3-time loser, which meant if convicted a fourth time for any crime, he would go away for life.

The fellow asked, "If I give you something good, can I walk?" He understood clearly what a fourth conviction would mean.

He was told, "If it's good enough, yes."

He said, "I know of an old lady coming in on a train with 2 bags, each with 2 kilos of heroin. If I give you the details, would that be good enough?"

"Yes, that would be good enough," he was told.

He asked for the commitment in writing, and after getting it, he told the detectives the details:

"She's coming in on Friday on the 3:30 train at the main train station. She'll be pushing a cart containing the drugs and lots of other things."

"Ok," the detectives said, "we'll stake it out, and if everything pans out, you can walk."

The detectives put this fellow in a holding cell until the Friday event took place.

The detectives went to the main train station and found out that the Friday 3:30 train was coming in on Track 5. They staked out Track 5 at the appointed time, and sure enough, an old lady walked off the train pushing a cart with what looked like all her worldly possessions.

The detectives stopped her, they had a warrant to search her cart, and they found the drugs. After confiscating the drugs, they escorted the old lady back to the police station, where she was incarcerated until arraignment.

The detectives brought the original fellow out of his holding cell and told him that since the event panned out, he could walk.

As this guy was leaving the police station, my friend whispered to him,

"How did you know about this?"

The fellow answered, "She's my mother."

THE TRIPLE TRACKS

Over thirty years ago, we were going to Florida for a week's vacation. 4 couples were leaving on a Saturday morning. But on Friday night, we started the vacation early by going out to dinner together.

We drove to my one friend's house and he'd drive us and his wife to the restaurant to meet the other 2 couples.

This friend is always tinkering with something. When we got to his house, he proudly announced that he got new windshield wipers. Triple tracks, he said, like on airplanes. We got in his car, and it had just started drizzling.

"Great! I can try out my triple tracks!"

He turned on the windshield wipers.

Streak, smear. Smear, streak.

"Damn!"

He took the old wipers out of the trunk and switched them. The old ones worked perfectly.

He grumbled all night.

Next day on the plane, I spoke to the flight attendant. When we landed in Florida, she came over the loudspeaker. "Welcome to Florida. By the way, this is to let everyone know that the triple tracks worked just fine." I saw my friend smile.

I heard the woman across the aisle and behind me say, panicky, "What's wrong with the triple tracks?"

That's why flight attendants don't make announcements like that until after we land.

THE BLOW DRYER

I blow dry my hair every morning. For decades I kept a backup blow dryer just in case.

One year I had a customer presentation. I wore a 3-piece suit. After showering, I got dressed and took out my blow dryer.

It didn't *work*!

That's why I have a backup.

Oh, *no*! My backup is broken *too*!

My wife said to call her friend up the block. She answered, but she said that she didn't use a blow dryer.

I called my friends who lived about a mile away. The wife had a blow dryer. I'll be right over.

I drove over with wet hair, wearing my 3-piece suit.

I knocked on their door. Their 15-year-old son answered the door. He knew our family, and he recognized me right away.

He looked at me incredulously and said, "What are *you* doing here?"

I replied, "I'm here to see your mother."

The son's carpool pulled up just then and he was the last one aboard. Several of the passengers saw me at our friends' house. They all knew us.

I never explained it to them.

I like being mysterious.

I now keep *two* backup blow dryers.

THE KOREAN WAR

When the game Trivial Pursuit was popular, we were playing against 3 other couples.

The game plodded along, and then this one couple reached the square where a roll of "6" on the die would land them in the center, and then they would need one correct answer to win.

They rolled a "6".

It was my turn to take the card and ask the question. I read the card and asked,

"What was the big event of 1950?"

That was an easy one. The Korean War.

I turned the card over to see the answer on the back, and I was correct.

The husband answered, "The Korean War." I was distraught internally. They would win. The game would be over.

Then the wife said, "No, I think it was television."

I perked up! The game *wasn't* over!

They argued back and forth, and then she said, "I think it was *silent* television."

(Yes, that's what she said!)

Now do you know how hard it is not to laugh at something while you keep a straight face? I thought I swallowed my tongue a few times.

They argued some more, and finally he caved. "Silent television it is," they said.

"No, it's the Korean War." I said.

You should have heard the screams.

I thought he would kill her.

BONANZA

In the following year, we were again playing Trivial Pursuit, this time with different friends. It was the wives against the husbands (he and I each have a PhD).

The ladies got to the center and they had to answer 1 question to win.

Once again, it was my turn to read the question. It asked the following:

What was the name of the Chinese cook on *Bonanza*? (This was years ago when the TV program *Bonanza* was very popular)

The ladies huddled for 10 minutes and offered many answers: Wo Fat; How Long; many answers, but never the right one.

We had a chance! (Sound familiar?)

Finally, we said, "Time's up. What's your answer?"

"Hop Sing," they said in unison.

They never mentioned that answer once during their 10-minute discussion.

But it was the right answer.

Why were we surprised?

SURPRISE 65TH BIRTHDAY

My wife and I were invited to a surprise 65th birthday party for a friend. We arrived well ahead of his returning home, as requested for the surprise. We parked near their house, since he wouldn't recognize our car.

We were all gathered in the house. After a while, someone said, "Quiet! He's coming!"

We were quiet until the door opened.

"Surprise!" we all yelled.

He had no idea this was going to happen. The surprise was complete.

After the surprise died down, we all got to talking. That's when my friend told us that he saw the doctor the previous day, and the doctor had given him a clean bill of health. The doctor also said that my friend was in the best shape of his life.

After the party was over, we were in the car going home when my wife said, "I don't think he's is in as good a shape as his doctor told him."

"Why?" I asked.

"I didn't like his color. He looked gray and pasty."

The next day, our friend fell over dead from a massive heart attack.

I asked my wife, "How's my color?"

THE REFERENCES

It was time to renew my personal data at work. I had to provide 3 references of people who had known me for a long time.

I gave 3 friends.

One was a disciplinarian at an elementary school.

Piece of cake.

The company investigator, a lady, made an appointment and showed up at my friend's school office. It was customary for our investigators to visit a person of reference at their place of business for an interview. It was supposed to be for asking him a few routine questions about me.

The first few questions were simple. Then the investigator asked,

"Do you know if Mr. Porter and his wife live within their means?"

"This conversation is over," he said officiously, and ushered the investigator lady out of his office.

He then called me to proudly tell me this story.

Just exactly *how* did he think this would help me keep my job?

THE STRIP JOINT

My wife and I went to a strip joint as a gag, with 2 other couples. I mean, really, who would go to a strip club with their wife if it wasn't a gag?

A gorgeous blonde took us to a table for 6. A few moments later another gorgeous blonde came over.

"Would you like a lap dance?" she asked.

My wife said, "Go ahead." I got *permission*??

So the blonde gave me a lap dance. At our table. Next to my wife. I have to tell you that when you're getting a lap dance with your wife sitting next to you, it's not the slightest bit interesting.

When the blonde finished with me, I gave her a dollar tip in the side of her g-string. Then she moved over and gave my next friend a lap dance. His eyes glazed over, and he was in another world.

When she finished with him, my other friend whispered, "Give her a tip."

The first friend pulled out his wallet and unzipped the compartments. Zip, zip, zip.

He pulled out a dollar. "Where ...?"

"In the side of the g-string," my other friend said.

After he gave the blonde her tip, he zipped his wallet back up. Zip, zip, zip.

His wife was laughing the hardest.

The next day we were all out at the club. My first friend and his wife came later. We were discussing the strip joint, laughing about the previous evening.

When the other couple arrived, my wife asked the wife, "How did you like the strip joint last night?"

She said, "Great. When we got home, it was the best sex we had in 15 *years!*"

THE PARKING SPOT

My long-standing friend of several decades passed away. But I remember the good times.

For example, the four of us were going to a Chinese restaurant in Chinatown. It was one of our favorite restaurants.

Since the city put in a nearby expressway, they had to change the local streets all through Chinatown and around the restaurant.

We saw a parking spot about half a block from the restaurant.

"Here's a good spot. It's only a half block away from the restaurant," I said.

"Don't park here," my friend said. "We'll get a closer spot."

I just looked at him.

But I did what he asked. I went around the block and came up the street where the restaurant was located.

A car pulled out right in front of the restaurant, and I got a parking spot right there, just like my friend said.

I've been going right to our destination ever since, and there's usually a parking spot right in front.

THE BALL COZY

For my 40th birthday, my wife threw me a party. Many of our friends were there.

As I opened my gifts, everyone cheered and clapped, as they usually do.

Then I got to one marked, "Open Last." My wife had set it aside. One of the other wives had made it.

When I opened it, it was a patriotic-looking red, white and blue knitted ball cozy.

I had never seen one before.

It was shaped like a cucumber, with two small sacks near the base.

Everyone figured out what it was for, and they all started hooting and hollering.

No wonder she marked it "Open Last." It was very appropriate that it was the last gift opened.

Later on, we were invited to a 50th surprise birthday party for a co-worker, at a country club. We asked our friend to make us another ball cozy as a gag gift, since we figured that none of my co-worker's family or friends would have seen it.

Our friend made us the gag gift.

We marked it, "Open Last."

There were almost 100 people at this party. When my co-worker exhausted his real gifts, he finally opened the one marked "Open Last."

Everyone figured out what it was for, and there was raucous laughter.

After the last gift was opened, 6 women came up to my wife and wanted to *order* one!

HEARING AND AGING

One summer, we were visiting our married friends in Atlantic City. They have a nice place there.

The husband told us that as he got older, he was having trouble hearing. So he went to a doctor to get tested.

The doctor looked at the test results and told my friend, "You have some reduction at high frequencies. This means that you can probably hear men better than women."

"Now I know why I can't hear my wife," my friend said as an aside.

Then my friend told us the following story:

"To fix the high frequency problem, I went out and got hearing aids. $6,000! They made everything sound tinny, so I couldn't wear them. I gave them back. That's when I decided that it wasn't so bad not hearing my wife."

When I recently told this story to a different friend, he told me that this is a common condition. It's known as Marital Deafness (similar to Marital Amnesia).

FIRST VISIT TO THE DELI

Years ago, our friends invited us to go to a local deli where everything was large. They also invited another couple who had gone with them before. The other couple met us at the deli.

My friend told me to bring a cooler. I asked why, since I never leave anything on my dinner plate.

Just bring it, he said. So I did.

We picked them up and went to this deli. We met their friends there, and we sat at a table for 6.

For the sandwiches, my wife likes corned beef and I like roast beef. "Why don't we get one of each?" she asked.

"I'll get corned beef with you this time," I said. "Our friend said the sandwiches are huge. Let's see how big they are before we order a second one."

We ordered one sandwich per couple. Large, not extra-large (only 2 sizes).

Our corned beef sandwich was at least 9 inches high, and there was no way to eat it all.

Everyone took home a lot of food. It reminded me of Dungeness crabs.

I understood what the cooler was for.

The big guy at the next table ordered one of those extra-large sandwiches. When it came it was so tall that it was wobbling on the plate. The waitress laid it on its side so it wouldn't fall over (I have a picture).

It was a real experience. I don't have stock in the deli, but I'm thinking about it.

OTHER VISITS TO THE DELI

We took our younger granddaughter to the same deli. She loved it. She walked around the restaurant taking pictures of the other people's food.

All *large* portions!

It turned out that the deli was also a full restaurant. They had lots of other things besides deli stuff. Spaghetti and meatballs, hot dogs, ribs. Everything large. Our granddaughter took pictures.

We saw one large guy get the ribs. When it arrived at his table, I heard someone say something about a "...side of beef." Even though the portion was huge, he ate it down to the bones.

One time we were going past the deli to a friend's event several hours away. It was a long ride, so we decided to stop at the deli for breakfast. We ordered pancakes. We asked if we could have chocolate chips in one half. The waiter said that we could.

But our order was a *mistake*! We should have ordered one pancake, but the waiter didn't remind us.

When the pancakes came, they were each the size of a large pizza. I ate a quarter of one pancake (with chocolate chips) and my wife ate another quarter plain. I said maybe we should take the rest with us in case we got hungry later.

The waiter brought out a large pizza box. The left-over pancakes (2½ of them) barely fit.

We forgot that at this deli everything is *LARGE*!!

HOT FOOD

One of my friend's at work was from the west coast, and he was into hot food.

Similar to what Colonel Troutman said in the movie *First Blood*, he would "…eat things that'd make a billy goat puke!"

He taught me about the Scoville scale (I looked up some of the details since I was the MC for his retirement roast). Jalapeños 2,500-8,000. Tabasco Sauce Habanero 7,000-8,000. And so on.

He took me to his favorite spice store and bought Dave's Insanity Sauce (DIS), 250,000 on the Scoville scale! Only one drop in an entire pot of stew!

Later he bought DIS II. 1,500,000 on the Scoville scale. The scale showed that pure capsaicin peppers top out at 16,000,000!

My friend brought in hot foods for our year-end pot-luck lunches. Good thing he labeled the hot ones! Only a taste!

When we were in Florida, my wife and I saw a hot food store. I went in to buy my friend a gag gift.

I had to sign a release before the store would sell it to me.

I bought the gag gift because of the name.

Colon Cleaner.

My friend said it wasn't bad.

I think it would've taken paint off my car.

WORD GAMES

PLAYING BOGGLE

I taught my son how to play word games from age 9, when he got a Boggle set as a birthday present.

He now beats me silly.

During the process, when he was 12, we were playing Boggle with the very bright high school senior down the block (who's now a dean at a university – no surprise).

The senior played the word MOA.

"That's not a word," I said. "What does it mean?"

He said, "It's a large extinct ostrich-like bird from New Zealand."

Yeah, right.

We got the dictionary out.

The dictionary definition read, "a large extinct ostrich-like bird from New Zealand."

He had it verbatim.

We never questioned him again.

PSYCHOLOGY EXPERIMENT #1

My son volunteered for a psychology experiment when he was in college.

For this experiment, the teacher gave the class a set of 50 jumbled 5-letter words to unscramble.

Easy peasy, he thought, after all the word game stuff we were doing.

He got 49 right out of 50!

Of course he did. I *taught* him!!

The teacher said he had to throw out our son's result, since it was such an outlier.

What does a father ask?

"What was the one you got wrong?"

He misread one set of letters. He wrote "foray" instead of "foyer". He misread the "e".

He was 18.

Of course I remember.
So does he.

PSYCHOLOGY EXPERIMENT #2

For our son's next psychology experiment, the teacher gave out 3 groups of 7 letters with letter values like in Scrabble.

The assignment was to take each group of 7 letters and make as many words as possible. Then to determine the score for each word and add the scores to get that round's total.

A score of 300 for any round was exceptional.

Note that for this experiment, finding a 7-letter word did not get the 50-point bonus for being a Bingo, like in Scrabble. Only the word score counted.

Our son got the following scores:
Group 1:   407
Group 2:   452
Group 3:   511.

The teacher said he had to again throw out his results, since once more they were outliers.

PLAYING SCRABBLE #1

Henny Youngman told one of his famous comedic stories. "I went to a psychiatrist. The Doctor said, 'You're crazy.' I said, 'I need a second opinion.' The Doctor said 'You're ugly.'"

Once I started to get better at some word games, I decided to try Scrabble. So I entered a Scrabble tournament, and in one game I played the word ZEROES. I knew this was good, since ZERO can have either plural, S or ES.

My opponent challenged.

I knew he would lose.

The referee came over with the dictionary.

A challenger is not allowed to say *anything*. He simply writes the challenged word on a piece of paper.

The referee looked at the piece of paper, and he looked up the word. He could say only "Acceptable" or "Unacceptable."

The referee said, "Unacceptable."

I knew he was wrong. Players have recourse if they believe a referee has made a mistake. You can call the tournament referee and ask for a review.

I raised my hand and said the only words that can summon the tournament referee: "Second opinion."

Most of the room yelled, "You're ugly!"

They obviously heard Henny Youngman's famous story.

PLAYING SCRABBLE #2

Once my son became proficient in our household word games, I took him with me to the local Scrabble club.

For one of his games (there are usually 4), he wound up playing a lady who was at one time the best female Scrabble player in our state (she was also state champion). This lady had forgotten more than I will ever know.

Playing her would be tough for my son, I thought. At least he might learn something.

After we finished that round of games, my son and I talked about his game with the lady champion.

"So who won?" I asked, expecting the obvious.

"I did," he said rather nonchalantly.

I glared at him.

"How in the world did you do *that*?"

"I played the word LOZENGES with a double word score, and I scored over 90 points for this Bingo. The lady had a lot of high-scoring plays after that, and she almost caught up. It was close at the end."

But he pulled it out!
How proud can a father be?

CATEGORY 8

GRANDCHILDREN

FIRST GRANDCHILD

At 35 weeks, our daughter went into labor early. She was in labor for almost 5 days.

The doctors decided to do an amniocentesis (a needle into the uterus to withdraw fluid) to see if an enzyme showed that the baby's lungs were working.

A risky procedure, but they had to do something. When the enzyme was present, they induced labor.

But labor wasn't forthcoming.

The 4 parents were dismissed to wait at the kids' house. We showered and got into bed at 12:30 AM. Then the phone rang. You better come back.

We all jumped out of bed, dressed, and rushed to the maternity waiting room. It was 1:45 AM.

His mother paced back and forth for a long time. Then she saw a man walking in the nearby corridor.

She ran over to him and asked, "Any *news*?"

"Lady, I'm the janitor."

At 3:45 AM, our son-in-law came out and told us, "It's a girl! She's beautiful!" We went in and saw the new arrival. Beautiful? What's he *talking* about?

Face bruised. Head squashed. Forehead slanted.

"Isn't she just *gorgeous*?" one of the doctors said.

After we saw the baby, I had to go to work. In the car, I said, "Did you see the same thing I saw?"

"Yes," my wife replied. "The baby looked beaten up! Thank G-d they know the plastic surgeons!"

We went back the next evening. "She's *gorgeous* today!" my wife exclaimed. "How did that happen?"

A just-born baby looks like that. In 24 hours, the same baby will look completely different.

GRANDDAUGHTERS

When my daughter was pregnant with her second baby, we had our first granddaughter for the day.

She was 20 months old.

We took her to several places to keep her busy, including children's stores and then various stores in the mall.

For her difficult second pregnancy, our daughter had to be on bed rest. We had to take our first granddaughter (in her parents' van since they had the baby equipment already mounted in the back seat) to see her mother in the hospital.

When we arrived in the hospital parking lot, our granddaughter looked up, saying, "Mommy's house."

When we left the hospital after visiting her mother, she said, "Mall please."

Another time, our daughter took our first granddaughter to the mall for lunch. Our granddaughter fell off the bench and hit her head on the concrete floor.

The next time we visited, my wife asked our granddaughter, "What happened to you at lunch?"

She said, "I fell and hit my head on the mall."

THE BOTTLE

When our daughter was still pregnant with her second, we were visiting her home (about 4 hours away by car) for a holiday dinner. Our first granddaughter was then 21 months old. Our son-in-law's sister and her family were also there for the holiday dinner. She had a boy a month after our first granddaughter was born, and then she had her second boy 18 months later. He was then 2 months old.

The boy was in a rocking seat, sucking on a bottle. Our granddaughter went over to her cousin and looked at him rocking. We were standing right next to her and talking, and we could see everything.

Our granddaughter pulled the bottle out of his mouth, and he began wailing. I mean, *screaming*! She immediately pushed the bottle back into his mouth, and the wailing stopped.

She turned toward us and smiled.

We stopped talking and watched.

Then she turned back to him and pulled the bottle out again. More wailing, maybe even louder. She pushed the bottle back in a second time, and the wailing stopped again.

She turned to look at us, and then she smiled this impish little smile. Without turning back to look at her cousin, our granddaughter reached backwards and pulled the bottle out again. When he began wailing, she just kept smiling.

Our granddaughter had just performed her first scientific experiment.

MOVING HOME

When our daughter was nearing the delivery of her second child, she and her family decided to move back to our area. We figured they wanted the built-in babysitters (that's us). We were right!

They bought a house while our daughter was in the hospital with her difficult second pregnancy, without her seeing it. Our son-in-law and I went to see the various places, and he videoed them so our daughter could get the gist. After seeing the video of their current house, she gave the okay from her hospital bed.

Our daughter delivered her second daughter, and then they were moving into their new home in our area. That's when our daughter finally saw the new house.

When the movers were moving them in, we again had our first granddaughter for the day. She was almost two years old. We took her to lunch, and then did some things with her, and then dinner.

We brought her home at 7:30 PM.

The movers had finished installing the furniture, but the boxes hadn't been unpacked. They were everywhere.

My wife asked our first granddaughter, "How do you like your new house?"

She replied, "It's *messy!*"

BRINGING BABY HOME

After our daughter brought her second daughter home, it was a wonderful time of our lives. The family had moved into the new house, and we knew that our baby-sitting job had just begun.

The new baby sister did what babies did. She ate, pooped, cried and slept.

One time in the new house, our daughter was changing the baby's diaper. The older sister showed her curiosity and just had to see what was going on. When our daughter had the baby's diaper open, the older sister stuck her face in to see everything.

Her head snapped back and she exclaimed, "*That* is a poopy ex*pwo*sion!"

Today, our first granddaughter no longer has any difficulty with "L's" and "R's." In fact, she has no trouble talking at all!

A 2-YEAR-OLD's VIEW

When our first granddaughter was a little over 2 years old, the family had moved into their new house. All the boxes had been emptied and everything was put away.

When we visited, our first granddaughter took my finger and said, "Pop-pop, come sit with me in the car."

The car?

Then she pulled me into the other oom and we sat on a sofa. She took her tray from the highchair, put it across her lap, and attached a steering wheel with suction cup to the metal tray. Then she attached a mirror also with suction cup to the tray.

"Where are we going?" I asked.

"Nordstrom's," she replied. She was 2 years old.

Really?

After swallowing the laughter, I asked, "What are we going to get there?"

"Outfits."

When my granddaughter finished with me a little while later, I walked out to the other room and found our daughter. I said to her,

"Do you remember when we said, 'Someday you'll get pay-back for all the aggravation you gave us? And pay-back's a bitch?'"

"Yes?" my daughter said looking at me quizzically.

"She's in the other room." I replied.

DIAPER CHANGE

At one point, our granddaughters were 2½ years old and 6 months old.

At that time, our daughter could tell that one of the girls needed a diaper change.

"Which one of you has to be changed?" she asked to herself, but unfortunately her thought came out verbally.

The older one stuck her face into the back of the baby's diaper. When her head snapped back, she exclaimed,

"We have a *winner!*"

GROWING PAINS

When our older granddaughter was 3 years old, her parents were delighted that she finally got potty trained!

Until you have a child that needs potty training, you cannot completely understand.

A few days later, we all went to a family event, and there were 150 people there, including many children. Our 3-year-old was standing with her friend who was 3½ years old.

We were standing nearby, when we heard our granddaughter tell her friend, "I finally got potty trained."

"You *did*?" the friend said excitedly.

"Yes!" our granddaughter exclaimed. "See?"

Our granddaughter pulled up her dress and said,
"Big girl underpants!"

Her friend grabbed her and hugged her hard, exclaiming,
"You're such a big *girl* now!"

THE BOARDWALK

When our granddaughters were 6 and 4, we all went to Atlantic City's beach for the day. We had just come off the beach and were looking to get lunch for the girls.

So we got them a hamburger for the older one and a hot dog for the younger one.

When we put the plates down in front of them, a sea gull swooped down and scooped the younger one's hot dog right out of the bun!

She started wailing. "The mean bird took my hot dog!"

"Don't worry," my wife said, trying to calm her down. "We'll get you another hot dog."

I ran to the hot dog stand and got another one. Then I brought it to the table and placed it in front of our younger granddaughter.

She huddled over the hot dog with both arms around the plate, and she said,

"I'm gonna make sure that mean bird doesn't get my hot dog this time!"

She ate the entire replacement hot dog within her arm cocoon. No way that 'mean' bird could get at it!

THE RAINFOREST CAFÉ

For her 10th birthday, we took our older granddaughter to dinner at the Rainforest Café on the Atlantic City boardwalk.

She loved the place.

When dinner was over, we took her out onto the boardwalk, and there were several rolling chairs by the railing. We decided to sit on one of the chairs until the driver told us to get up.

We watched the people going by on the boardwalk for almost a half hour. Very few chairs were in use, so the driver didn't bother us.

As we continued to people-watch, I said to her, "Do you want to know the secret about people?"

"What's the secret, Pop-Pop?"

"Don't tell anyone, but most people are ugly."

"Oh, *Pop*-Pop!" she sneered.

Another 15 minutes went by as we watched more people on the boardwalk.

Then she said, "You know, Pop-Pop, you're *right*!"

We never talk about how people look. Instead, our granddaughter just says, "Pop-Pop, do you remember what you told me in Atlantic City?"

Seems to come up every so often.

FOUR GRANDDAUGHTERS

We have friends whose children are friendly with our children and whose granddaughters are friendly with our granddaughters. Each pair of girls was close in age, around 10 years old and separated by about 2 years.

One night, the parents allowed the grandparents to take the granddaughters to a Chinese restaurant for dinner. Without the parents!

New territory for both my wife and our daughter!

A store for sex toys had opened next door to the Chinese restaurant. We didn't know that the store had opened, or we would have gone elsewhere.

When dinner was over, all 4 girls went to the ladies' room. Then they came running out.

"Come to the ladies' room!" they exclaimed. My wife and the other grandmother went to look. The girls pointed to a sign above the toilet. "No needles, no condoms." The girls were all giggling.

We figured that the store next door had something to do with it.

Then I heard the grandmothers talking. One said to the other, "When the girls tell their parents about this, I hope our children will let us take the girls out again."

COMPUTER EXPERTISE

When our 2nd granddaughter was 10, she was a 4-sport threat (softball, basketball, soccer, field hockey). Not only that, both girls were well versed in the Apple computer products, since they used several of them at home.

It turned out that all the kids their ages were well versed in the Apple products.

Our daughter and her husband took their older daughter to an event on a Saturday, and we had the younger one for the day. We had to pick the younger one up at noon after her softball game ended.

"What do you want to do? Go to lunch?" I asked.

"Nahhhh…"

"Go to a movie?"

"Nahhhh…"

"I have to get a new computer. Would you like to go to Best Buy and help me get one?"

"Oh, *boy*, Pop-Pop! Let's *go!*"

Then she said something I will never forget. "What could be better than being surrounded by a bunch of electronics!"

When we got to Best Buy, she made a bee-line to the large-screen MAC computer, which they had at home. She knew I don't use Apple computers, so she began to give me a tutorial on the features of the MAC. After a few minutes of that, a Geek Squad guy came by and observed what she was doing.

"Need any help?" he said to me.

"I don't think so. We have our own expert with us," I joked.

"I see what you mean," he said.

Then I turned to him and jokingly asked, "Any chance of getting her a summer job?"

"Not this summer, but maybe next year. I'm the manager here, and she seems to know more about that computer than my Geek Squad guys."

AMSTERDAM TO BRUGGE

We took our older granddaughter to Amsterdam, Brugge and Paris for her birthday. To get from Amsterdam to Brugge, we took the train. It wasn't a direct ride. We took a bullet train to Brussels, a large Belgian station, and then we switched to a local train to Brugge.

When I got the trip itinerary from the travel agent, I saw that we had 4 minutes between trains at the Brussels train station. That seemed awfully short, so I called the agent.

The agent said, "I saw that too, so I checked. They told me the Europeans do that all the time."

So we stayed with the itinerary. My wife and I each took a large suitcase, and our granddaughter had a large duffel bag and a smaller suitcase.

When we got on the first train, our granddaughter fell up into the car on her duffel bag, laughing. She would fall into every train car on her duffel bag for the rest of the trip. It became a running joke.

On the bullet train to Brussels, I told the train conductor that we had a short time in Brussels. So when we were arriving, he moved all our suitcases to the door to make sure we could get off quickly. Then he told me to find the station master, who'd know the track for the train to Brugge.

We got off and had all our suitcases in a pile on the platform. The station master said that the Brugge train was on Level 6. We were on Level 1.

We saw people getting off an elevator. We ran over there and my wife held the elevator while I got our luggage. But the elevator only went to Level 4.

When we got off the elevator, there was a stairway to Level 6 next to the elevator. We had to get the luggage up 2 flights to Level 6.

I started up with our 2 large suitcases, but I couldn't lug them all the way. They were too heavy together. I had to leave one suitcase on the landing halfway up and take the other suitcase to Level 6. Then I came back for the second suitcase.

The girls watched me from Level 4, and then I ran down and helped them with the smaller suitcases.

On Level 6, we asked a passerby which train went to Brugge, and he pointed to one of the 2 trains waiting on both sides of the platform. We threw all the luggage on that train and then we got on, hoping for the best.

I flopped into a seat, hoping not to have a heart attack, and the train immediately left the station. Not a moment to spare. The electronic sign above the door to the next car said 'Brugge.' Luckily, we were on the correct train.

The Europeans do this all the time?

It turned out there was an elevator that went to Level 6. It was around the corner, but we couldn't see it when we got off the bullet train.

I figured that the Europeans had no luggage, and they knew where the elevator to Level 6 was.

It also turned out that the local trains to Brugge ran every 30 minutes.

No one told us *that* either.

NOISES

When our grandsons each turned 5 years old, they had to get glasses.

One of them had a habit of making noises at the dinner table. His mother told him many times not to make those noises.

When we were there for dinner one night, the older grandson was making those noises again. My wife (his grandmother) said to him,

"You know your mother doesn't want you to make noises."

He looked up at my wife over the top of his glasses and said,

"I think I can see where you're going with this."

Analytical as usual.
Lawyer? Engineer?

ACTION FIGURES

When our older grandson was around 7 years old, he was being bad in some fashion. His mother had to punish him for that.

She said, "You're being bad! I'm taking away your action figures!"

He replied without any hesitation, "How many? Are you taking the good ones? When do I get them back?"

We call him 'The Negotiator.'

Lawyer, definitely.

CRUISES

We took our granddaughters (then ages 14 and 12) on a cruise in a 2-bedroom suite with a butler. It cost about the same as 2 separate cabins.

We never used the butler, but the girls did. A lot! They ordered breakfast and ate in every day, while we went walking. When we came back from our walks, we found them lying about in their robes, eating whatever breakfast they had ordered from the butler.

Pancakes with syrup. Omelets. Orange juice. Little chocolates.

We're the grandparents. We're supposed to spoil them.

The butler even brought them shrimp later in the day as an afternoon snack.

When we got back home after the cruise, our daughter and her husband had an event to attend, and we were with the girls again.

This built-in babysitter thing was working quite well for our daughter.

We took the girls to dinner at a Chinese buffet. After finishing our dinners, my wife and I were talking about our next cruise, when the older granddaughter perked up.

"You're going on another cruise?" she asked. "I'm *in!*"

MORE TRIPS

We had been on several vacations with our daughter and her family, and as I mentioned before, we even got to take her girls by ourselves.

When her younger daughter was 14, the next-door neighbor's grandparents died, and she got worried about us.

She told us, "We have to go on more trips while we still can." We thought that was a little morbid.

A few moments later, she said, "Oh, well, "I guess I'll get it in the inheritance anyway."

THE ELECTRONICS STORE

We took our grandsons (brothers) to a store where they sold all kinds of electronic gadgets.

One brother was eying an item closely. His mother (our daughter-in-law) had given him both gift cards and cash, since she knew where we were taking the boys.

She never presumes that we will pay for the boys' stuff, and she always gives them enough money for their needs.

My wife noticed the dilemma playing out in the one grandson's mind. How much the item cost, and how much he had to spend.

It was a good lesson on how to manage your money. His mother thinks of things like that.

My wife said, "Sweetie, it looks like you want that item. Take it to the cashier and we'll get it for you."

"Really?" he said incredulously.

"Yes, we'll buy it for you."

Instead of taking the item and going to the left toward the cashier, he turned the other way and ran to the other end of the store, where his brother was looking at another item.

"Get something!" he yelled. "They're *paying*!"

RUBE GOLDBERG MACHINE

When our older granddaughter was in 8th grade, she was on a team that had to build a Rube Goldberg machine. The machine had to transfer energy many times, finishing with a hammer pounding a nail.

The team set out to build the machine, but after 60 tries, they had only failures. They had 1 week left.

So our granddaughter took it on herself to take home what they'd done so far on the project, and try to finish it in time herself. She videoed the machine in action, since their final presentation would be a video created from 3 recording devices: her camera, her iPhone, and her iPad, all shot at different angles.

She called me for some help, and I went there. The machine funneled a ball into a cup. Then the ball fell into a race on a table. At the end of the race, the ball knocked over dominoes that knocked larger items over until a truck was rolled off the table, pulling a weight to rotate the hammer onto the nail.

We adjusted the machine several times, but we still had 39 more failures. The ball got stuck in the funnel, the ball fell out of the race, and so on.

On the 100th try, after about 3 hours, the machine worked!

The videos had sound, and you could clearly hear my granddaughter cheering in the background as the hammer came down on the nail head on the 100th try.

She was only 13, but she didn't get rattled by failure. Instead, she analyzed each case and saw what was needed to improve the process.

Wish I had more engineers like that when I worked!

THE SIGNATURE

My granddaughters both call me Pop-Pop. (So do my grandsons. It makes everything easier that they all call me the same thing.)

Our second granddaughter was taking a high school course in Calculus. Very advanced.

I'm a retired engineer, which means I used a good deal of math in my career. Knowing that, my second granddaughter created a t-shirt for me that says on the front,

$$d/dPop \ (1/3 \ Pop^3)$$

and on the back

$$\int 2 * Pop * dPop$$

Both of these mathematical terms result in Pop^2, or Pop-Pop.

So far only one person has understood the math. He was the chairman of my thesis committee when I was getting my PhD. He now lives in my condo complex, and when I showed this to him, he knew what the terms reduced to, immediately.

I now sign my text messages to my granddaughters with the first term.

I am a retired engineer who is blessed.

IDENTITY

I used to have an identity of my own.

    I was an engineer.

    I was a corporate Fellow.

    My company valued my inputs.

    I knew who I was.

    Now that I've retired, I'm only *their* grandfather.

    But I'm getting used to it.

PERSONAL

SELLING HEALTH FOOD

Part 1

Several decades ago I was on the board of my athletic club.

My in-laws ran a luncheonette. When they retired, we took their long counter and installed it in our club. We did that so my in-laws would come to periodic tournaments and sell hot dogs, hamburgers and steak sandwiches, to make extra cash in retirement.

One of our players saw their process working. He decided to build a small booth and sell health food to the athletes.

After a major tournament, I was driving everyone home when my father-in-law said, "J.L., you're not going to believe this (I think his comment was the precursor to this book)."

"What do you mean?" I asked.

"Your friend asked me for some advice. I told him I would be glad to help. What do you need?"

He said, "Well, I don't seem to be making any money selling health food to the athletes."

"What are you selling?" I asked.

"Fruits, nuts, bananas, hard-boiled eggs. You know, health food."

"So tell me," I said. "For example, what do you pay for hard-boiled eggs?"

"$1.20 a dozen."

"What are you selling them for?
"A dime."
(Rule #1)

Part 2

My friend retired a short while later, and about a year after that I received a phone call from him.

"J.L., I finally figured out what I can do in retirement."

"What's that?"

"I'm in a new business," he replied.

"What's your new business?" I asked hopefully.

"Estate planning."

(Rule #1, squared)

I politely declined.

EXPENSIVE DINNER

About forty years ago, a friend told me the following story.

A young man had dropped his date off at her house and was on his way home when he ran into one of his friends. He said to his friend, "I don't understand why it's so expensive to take a lady out to dinner."

"How much was dinner for the two of you?" his friend asked.

"$150."

"Wow, that's a lot (it *was* back then, but currently it's just a nice dinner)! Where did you take her?"

The young man mentioned a local restaurant.

"I know that restaurant," his friend said. "It shouldn't have cost that much there. Did you each have lobster and an expensive bottle of wine?"

"No. We had regular dinners. And no liquor."

"And the bill was still $150? For a regular meal?"

"No. The bill came to $75, and I tipped the bill."

It turned out that the young man didn't understand percentages.

THE GIANT RAT

I was playing at my athletic club when the club phone rang (before cell phones).

The person who answered ran over to me frantically. "It's your wife. Sounds like an emergency."

I grabbed the phone. "What's wrong?" I yelled.

My wife said, "There's a giant *rat* in the house! Come home right away!"

"I'll be there as soon as I can!"

I hung up, grabbed my stuff and bolted for the car. I drove home as fast as I could.

When I got home, I took my tire iron out of the trunk as a weapon and I ran inside. I found my wife standing on the dishwasher (a standalone machine) in the kitchen.

"When did you see the giant rat?" I yelled, brandishing the tire iron.

"Just before I called you."

"Where is it now?"

"I don't know. It's out there somewhere," pointing to our living room.

"How big is it?" I asked.

She held her fingers up and apart.

About 2 inches! A little mouse!

We searched the house, but we never did find the 'giant' rat! It turned up the next morning in one of the small mouse traps we had set.

HAVE-A-HEART TRAPS

When our kids were young, I was having a catch with our son behind our house. He threw the ball into the louvers to the attic and broke them.

It was an accident. No big deal, I thought.

Later we had squirrels in the attic. They gained access through the broken louvers.

The game warden brought us "Have-a-Heart" traps to catch them. That way, we wouldn't have to kill the squirrels. You put peanut butter inside the traps, and when the squirrel goes in and takes the peanut butter, it springs the door closed.

The fastest way to get rid of the problem was to dispose of the squirrels. But our kids wouldn't hear of that!

The option was to transport the trap over some water source (like a creek). That's so the squirrel inside the trap wouldn't be able to find its way home across a water barrier once released.

We caught the first of the squirrels, and we took the trap and squirrel to a mall 20 miles away. We put the trap on the ground, we pointed it away from our car, we stood at the other end of the trap, and we lifted the door. The squirrel took off in a straight line, heading in the opposite direction.

The kids were happy that we didn't have to kill the squirrel.

We did the same thing with the other squirrels we caught. None of them ever came back.

We fixed the louvers, but not before we caught all the squirrels.

TOURNAMENT ENTRY

I was part of running major tournaments for our club on the east coast of the USA.

I was the one taking entries for these tournaments, and many participants would try to enter after the entry deadline expired. I was the one who had the sorry task of telling them that the entries were closed.

That didn't stop some people, so I had to tell them entries were closed quite often.

One day we were running a major tournament, when I received an entry phone call from India. At least, the person speaking had an Indian accent.

In the case where someone was from the other side of the Earth, I was lenient with the deadline due to the time difference.

To make sure this player was on the other side of the Earth, I asked him where he was. I was thinking something like New Delhi, Bombay (back then), Calcutta, …

His response was totally unexpected.

He said, "In my living room," (with the Indian accent).

Whenever I ask my kids where they are, they both give that answer (with the Indian accent).

THE SIGMOIDOSCOPY

I was a manager at my company when I turned 45 years old. At the time, the company was giving free medical examinations to managers when they reached that age.

I went to the in-house doctor, and I told him that my mother had colon cancer. He suggested an in-house sigmoidoscopy, which is the examination of the lower colon. It was to be performed by a different company doctor in another building's medical office.

Seemed like a good idea to get checked.

I had to drink fluids to remove anything from my lower colon. Wasn't pleasant.

In the other medical office, I changed into a gown that was open in back. I spoke with the examining doctor at his desk. He had a book on his desk which he was getting published. The cartoon on the cover showed a bathroom, an open ceiling light fixture, a ladder on its side, and a man lying on the floor with his foot stuck in the toilet. He had obviously fallen off the ladder while changing a light. The book was titled *Everyone's an Asshole Sometimes!* (I couldn't find the book on the Internet. Never published?)

He had a sense of humor! I liked him!

The examining doctor then took me to an exam table, and I had to place my knees on the little platform at the end of the table, about 2 feet below the padded surface. He told me to lean forward and place my elbows on the pad.

Then my end of the table began to rotate upward, moving my rear end high into the air.

The doctor then inserted a long tube into my rectum. As it went in, he pumped air into my colon so he could see the surrounding tissues. All the while, he kept asking if I were okay.

Not comfortable at all, but I was okay.

He then said, "I've got good news and bad news."

Why would a doctor say that to someone whose mother had a history of colon cancer?

"The good news is that you're clear. The bad news is that you're not fully evacuated."

He then withdrew the long tube and lowered the table. When I got off, he handed me a plastic bottle with some more prep fluids.

"Drink this and let it do its thing. Then we'll finish your exam."

When I finished drinking and the fluids did their thing (about 3 hours), I went back to the medical area. Back on the little platform, rear end up in the air, long tube inserted again, more air pumped in.

Even more uncomfortable.

"Everything's clear," he said.

I turned my head back toward him. "Are you finished?"

"Yes, all done." He began withdrawing the tube.

"That's too bad," I joked. "I was beginning to enjoy this."

He looked at me suspiciously. Then he took out his notebook, and it looked like he was going to write something down.

"I'm *kidding*!" I yelled.

I guess he didn't have the sense of humor I thought he had.

EXASPERATING DRIVERS

I've seen all kinds of crazy drivers on the road. Cutting across several lanes, losing control of their car, running into other cars, and of course the slow drivers.

One Saturday morning I was heading into work for an 11:00 meeting, and I got behind a slow driver on a one-lane road. When we finally got to a 2-lane expressway, I passed the slow driver. As I passed him, I turned my head to look at the driver (before they had tinting) and said to myself,
"Yep, that's an asshole."

That night we went to a comedy club. The headliner comedian said,
"Slow drivers are a pain! Did you ever get behind a slow driver on a one-lane road? And when you finally passed that car, you looked in the car and said,
'Yep, that's an asshole!'"

Was he riding in my car that morning?

THE ENTERTAINMENT BOOK

Many years ago, we had the Entertainment Book for discount dining. The restaurants used this medium for advertising for future dining.

All of our friends had it too. And we all used it.

So six couples went in town to a well-known restaurant on a Saturday night.

It was a beautiful place.

We had reservations for 12 people, and there was no problem. Until we said we all had the Entertainment Book. The manager told us that the restaurant honored the Entertainment Book on Saturday night, but they could only honor tables for six people or less.

Two tables of six? Near each other?

No problem. That would work for all of us.

What happened next is hard to believe. They put 2 rectangular tables for 6 together, end to end. Not bad, right? Then they put a table for 2 between us.

(Yes, they did!)

After about ten minutes of the 12 of us talking through the couple between us, the couple suggested moving to the end of one of our tables, and we could slide together.

We quickly agreed, and then we bought them drinks and dessert.

The manager made a terrible business decision, especially what he did to those 2 people. The food was wonderful, but the 12 of us never went back.

I suspect neither did the couple who was placed between us.

So much for the advertising.

GEISHA DINNER

When I was in my 30s I had a perm (I have pictures). During that period I went to Tokyo, Japan, on business with 4 other people, including my friend/mentor.

I made a detailed technical presentation to our Japanese customer, explaining how a problem occurred on the hardware we sold them, and how we would fix it for future orders. The Japanese customer liked our presentation so much that their top 3 executives took the 5 of us to an expensive Geisha house for dinner.

There were several Geisha ladies sitting with us as we ate. There was one lady for each of us.

The Geisha lady (approximately 50 years old) who was sitting next to me undid my tie and took it off. Then she unbuttoned my shirt.

The Geisha ladies were all giggling.

I didn't know where this was going, but my 4 colleagues looked on with anticipation.

It turned out my Geisha lady was looking to see if my chest had curly hair like my perm.

My colleagues were so disappointed!

My mentor re-told that story several times, including the part where he talked about the Geisha lady who sat with him. "She had a horse face."

DINNER IN TOKYO

I went to Tokyo for another business trip, this time by myself. While I was there, I went out for dinner and found a MacDonald's. I didn't go in.

Then I found a typical Japanese place, and I did go in. It was long and narrow, with a long counter down the center. The cooks were on the other side of the counter, and customers sat along my side of the counter.

I sat down near the door. There was a plate in front of each customer seat, and an open-mouthed fish head figurine next to the plate.

One cook brought something I didn't like the looks of, and I waved him off.

He gave me a funny look.

The next thing the cook brought was something I recognized, and I took it. It was on a long toothpick. I ate it, and then I looked down the counter and saw a Japanese man doing the same thing. Then he put the toothpick in the fish head's mouth. So I put my toothpick in my fish head's mouth.

Was the fish head a receptacle for trash?

The cook kept bringing various items, and I waved off the ones I didn't like. Each time I did that, the cook gave me a dirty look.

I ate the ones I could recognize, and when I was finished eating there were several toothpicks in my fish head's mouth.

It turned out that you paid by the toothpick. The fish head wasn't for trash.

They also expected you to take every item.

What did I know?

ANOTHER STRIP JOINT

Several decades ago, 8 of us were on the way back from dinner in a restaurant across the river. We were in one couple's station wagon, and we stopped at a strip club on that side of the bridge. We went there again as a gag.

My wife and I happened to go in first, and as we reached for the door, someone opened it and walked out. It was my college classmate.

My wife also knew him, and assuming his wife was also there as a gag, she said, "Where's your wife?"

He replied, "She's at the nutcracker."

Two years later I threw a surprise party for my wife's birthday. My classmate and his wife were there, and so were the other 3 couples from the strip joint. One of the guys from that night, a real kibitzer, saw my classmate sitting on a sofa by himself. He recognized him from the strip joint.

When I saw the kibitzer sit down next to him, I heard the kibitzer say, "You look very familiar."

I could feel the danger immediately.

Fortunately, my friend the kibitzer didn't push it any further, and luckily, my classmate didn't remember the other 6 people from that fateful night.

I told my wife about the kibitzer's comment after the party.

We still laugh about it.

THE BARIUM ENEMA

My son was a radiology resident at a local hospital.

I needed another colon checkup, so I went to a colo-rectal doctor who taught my son in medical school.

Same process. Gown, open in back. Socks.

"Everything's clear," he said. "Is there anything else bothering you?"

"Well, every once in a while, I get a little pain in my side after playing tennis."

He looked at me.

"You're going for a barium enema. I know your son, and nothing's going to happen to you on my watch."

Will I ever tell him anything else?

At least I'll have a baseline.

So where should I get this barium enema? My son is at a local hospital. Why not ask him.

My son suggested doing it at his hospital, since his attending performed most of the barium enemas at my son's hospital.

I scheduled the procedure.

I had to drink a liquid for prep, and then I emptied out. I left for the hospital, and when I got there, I had to put on a gown, open in back. And socks. I understood the process.

I walked into the room where they did the barium enema procedure, and there were these 2 gorgeous female technicians.

It turned out that my son had gotten the 2 best looking technicians in the department for my test.

I took one look at them, and at any other time this would have been rather pleasant.

But not then.

"I have absolutely no interest in these girls now," I said to my son. "But I will get even with you for this."

When the procedure ended, I went to the bathroom, eliminated the fluid, and got dressed. Then my son had his attending explain the results.

"Since you're my intern's father, I'll give you a full tutorial, if you're interested."

"Sure," I said. "I'm an engineer. It would be very interesting."

He showed me my films, and he said that my colon is what they're all supposed to look like. It was like a long tube made of attached marshmallows.

Then he showed me a bad one. Lots of black in the film. I understood why someone would need to get their colon checked out.

My son was getting off his shift, and I felt good enough to join him for lunch. We went to a pizza place across the street from the hospital.

A nice day for a proud father.

But during lunch I had to run to the bathroom again. My son said, "That's normal. They pump in lots of solution during the procedure. You may need to do that some more. Go home after this."

We finished lunch, and I felt empty. I figured that instead of going home, I'd go back to work. A 20-minute drive out the expressway. No big deal.

Big mistake!

On the expressway back to work, I was close to an exit when I had a violent urge to go back to the bathroom. But traffic stopped!

Is this for real?

I had no idea where a bathroom would be at that exit. But I needed only 10 minutes more on the expressway to get to work. I knew that a bathroom was located right by the entrance to my plant.

So I waited for traffic to start moving, and when it cleared, I passed the exit and booked it to work.

I parked in the lot and ran in the door.

Oh, *no*! The bathroom was out of order!

And I had to *go*!

I knew where the next bathroom was, about a block away down the main hallway, nearer my office. I ran down there and just made it into a stall.

What relief!

When I finished, I went to my office, passing my program manager on the way.

"Are you okay?" he asked. "You look a little green."

I said I was all right, and I went into my office and sat down.

The next thing I knew was that it was about an hour later. I had fallen asleep at my desk.

I never did that before or after that day.

Should have gone home when I finished lunch, like my son said.

THE BERMUDA CRUISE

We took everyone on a cruise to Bermuda to celebrate my son's graduation from medical school, our daughter's anniversary, and our anniversary.

Pink sand beaches, beautiful country. We were all looking forward to it.

We had to make the reservations 6 months in advance, so we could get the cruise of our choice. We booked staterooms on a Norwegian Cruise Lines ship. I called my mother and I told her we were all going on a cruise to Bermuda on Norwegian Cruise Lines.

She was happy for all of us.

Six months went by, and it was time to leave for our cruise. I called my mother to say goodbye.

"Have a nice time in Norway," she said.

"Mom, we're not going to Norway. We're going to Bermuda on Norwegian Cruise Lines."

"That's good," she said. "I never understood why anyone would take a cruise to Norway."

THE COLONOSCOPY

One year we went to Spain for an anniversary vacation. This included a trip to see the Rock of Gibraltar. We'd heard about it all our lives.

See the monkeys at the top. They're all over the place, we were told. So we took a tour up to the top of the Rock, and there were the monkeys, as advertised.

The view from the top was breathtaking. We walked around and saw the surrounding area from every aspect. My camera was able to take panoramic pictures, and the pictures were breathtaking.

Then the bus took us back down to the town, and we did some more walking around.

We stopped into a jewelry shop. I bought my wife a pair of gold earrings for our anniversary.

She gave me a reciprocal anniversary present. She scheduled me for a colonoscopy.

(Yes, she did.)

Liquid prep, gown open in back. I knew the drill.

They give you an anesthetic, and you're out during the procedure. Better that way. It's much worse than getting a sigmoidoscopy (which I had previously).

I was all clear again.

But due to my family history, I've had colonoscopies every five years since. All clear each time.

I had one at age 75.
We scheduled another one when I'm 80.
The gift that keeps on giving.

THE NEW RESTAURANT

It was our son's birthday, and he was finishing his residency. We invited him to come out to where we lived, and we'd celebrate at the new restaurant that just opened.

It took an hour and 45 minutes to get seated (they'd been open only 3 weeks and they were still getting their act together), and I called for the manager. He came over, and after I explained this situation to him, he comped desserts.

We'd have preferred him comping dinner!

When the waiter came over, we ordered nachos for an appetizer. Then my wife ordered a chicken dish, our son ordered Thai chicken and peanuts, and I ordered angel hair pasta with shrimp. I also asked the waiter to bring the parmesan cheese and leave it on the table. He said he couldn't, but he'd come back as many times as necessary to give me more cheese.

The nachos came and we ate them. They were delicious! Then they brought 2 dinners, but not mine.

My wife and son smiled. They knew I get impatient.

My dinner finally came, and I saw red pieces in the angel hair pasta. The shrimp?

I picked at them. My wife knows me, and she whispered, "What's wrong?"

"I can't find any shrimp."

My wife and son started laughing.

I called the waiter over. He said, "Would you like some parmesan cheese?"

"No. I ordered angel hair pasta with shrimp, but I can't find the shrimp."

"Oh," he said. He grabbed my plate with his free hand and ran off.

By then my wife and son were laughing loudly.

The waiter brought my plate back. There were 6 large shrimp, tails up, in a clock-like pattern.

I picked one up and bit into it. It was cold.

"What now?" my wife asked.

I called the waiter over. He said, "Do you want parmesan cheese now?"

"No. These are cold."

"Oh. I'll get them nuked right away."

He grabbed my plate again, and he took off.

My wife and son were almost on the floor.

The waiter brought my plate back.

I stared at it.

"What now?" My wife was exasperated.

I called the waiter over. He said, "Do you want your parmesan cheese now?"

"No. There were 6 shrimp, I ate one, and now there are 4."

My wife and son were hysterical.

The waiter looked at me, then at the plate. Finally, he said, "They gave you too many shrimp the first time and had to take one back."

(Yes, he actually said that.)

My wife and son could barely breathe.

The waiter turned to go.

"Excuse me," I said.

"What's wrong *now*?!?" he exclaimed.

"Can I have some parmesan cheese?"

We took the comped desserts home.

THE STING RAY

My wife and I went on a cruise in the Caribbean. We took an excursion where we went to a sand bar in the middle of the ocean and swam with the sting rays.

Checked that off the bucket list.

The excursion people took video of all the passengers with the sting rays, one couple at a time. We bought a video (which we've never looked at).

One sting ray floated right up to my wife, and she held it from under its wings. She looked right into its eyes, and the sting ray maintained her gaze.

Later, my wife told me that her encounter with the sting ray was an emotional experience!

MY 60TH BIRTHDAY

When I turned 60, my wife threw me a surprise party.

My wife knew my mentor from work, and she asked him to roast me. He started the festivities by saying, "It's been my honor to work with such mediocrity..."

Then he said, "J.L. gave his wife the Kinardly diamond. You kinardly see it."

My son was the one who laughed hardest. It was at my expense, of course.

Later my mentor told the story of how a man went to the doctor. The doctor told him, "You have cancer, and you have Alzheimer's."
The man thought for a moment, and then he replied, "At least I don't have cancer."

Old stuff, but still funny.

My mentor was terrific at my surprise party.

THE NEW SECRETARY

My daughter got a position in a large facility in the suburbs, once they came back to our area. In this new position, secretaries would come and go.

So I had a little game I played with each new secretary.

I would call and ask for my daughter, Dr. Porter. The new secretary would always say, "May I ask who's calling?"

I would answer, "Dr. Porter." I have a PhD in Engineering.

She would pause, then say, "One moment."

My daughter figured out what I was doing, and the secretary would get back on the phone and say, "May I ask, which one?"

My son is also Dr. Porter. He's a radiologist.

"Tell my daughter that it's her father on the phone."

WORST PATIENT

I was an anal engineer when I was working.

I admit it freely.

I've retired, but I think I'm still anal.

My eyes were everything, since what I did as an engineer was all about numbers, designs, and pictures.

For many decades, I've been very picky about getting the prescription for my glasses right.

My optometrist is a lady to whom I've been going for over 3 of those decades. She knows all about my pickiness, and the reason I keep going back to her is that she knows how picky I am, and she's okay with it.

She's been getting my prescription right all this time.

On one visit, she told me that in her optometry class they told the students that their worst patient would be a nearsighted engineer.

Then she met me.

She said they had no idea.

THE F-WORD AND GROWING UP

One of my doctors shared 2 stories about her youngest daughter with me.

For the first story, the doctor and her youngest daughter were visiting the doctor's sister and the sister's son (the little girl's cousin). The little girl ran up to the doctor's sister and said, "My cousin said a bad word!"

Her aunt, not to let this go, replied, "What did he say?"

"He said the *F*-word!"

Now you may think that this would be enough for most adults, but not the daughter's aunt! So the aunt continued, "What's the F-word?"

The girl replied, "Bullshit!"

For the second story, the doctor had the day off on a Tuesday, and she took her younger daughter to school. The doctor wanted to speak with the teacher to see how her daughter was doing.

When she walked in, the teacher said to the doctor, "Come take a look. You have to see this!"

It turned out that the children had to write down (with assistance, since they weren't so good with letters yet) what they wanted to be when they grew up.

The doctor was thinking what could her daughter have written … teacher, doctor, lawyer, fire fighter, baseball player, etc.

She looked at what her daughter had written:

Debt Collector!!

RETIREMENT DAY

My wife was Executive Director of a non-profit organization for almost 18 years. She had streamlined the work, and to save them money, she cut back to 3 days a week.

However, as the boards changed, it was difficult to deal with each new set of personalities.

"I can't stand it anymore! I'm going to retire!"

"Bear with it," I would say. "You'll know the day when you really mean it."

The nonsense continued, and one day, my wife came home from work on a Thursday.

"You remember when you said that I'd know the day when I should retire?"

"I remember," I replied.

"It was Wednesday (yesterday)."

"Why don't you think about it over the weekend?" I asked.

"I don't have to think about it. I'm retiring."

After the weekend, nothing had changed. So she generated her retirement letter that Sunday night and took it into the organization on Monday morning.

I recommended that she give them 2 weeks' notice. In the letter she gave them a month's notice.

The president of the non-profit came in on Tuesday and read her retirement letter.

"What can I do to change your mind?" he asked.

"Nothing."

Since she retired, she's said many times that I was right (please write that down). 2 weeks' notice would have been better.

BANG!

I recently turned 75. The last automobile accident I had was over 45 years ago, where someone hit me in the back end of the car while I was standing in traffic.

A few months ago, I was going to physical therapy at 2 PM for a tennis injury, and I had just finished a different appointment. I headed onto the expressway, and traffic stopped where the lanes merged, as usual.

Bang!

I was rear-ended.

I got out of the car, and I asked the lady who was driving the van that hit me, "Are you all right?"

"Yes. I'm so sorry. I was distracted."

I said, "We can't stand here in the middle of the expressway. Can we drive farther down and pull over to exchange information?"

She agreed. We drove down the road and pulled over where the shoulder was wider.

I got her information, and then I went to my physical therapy appointment. On the way, I called the body shop I had used before, since it was near the physical therapy office.

After therapy, I got an estimate from my body shop for the repairs. $1,120!

When I got home, my wife reminded me that we had dinner plans, and I hurried to get dressed so we could get to our friends' house for dinner.

On the way we were stopped in traffic.

Bang! Rear-ended again!

No accidents for 45 years, and then twice in 3 hours! Both while I was standing still in traffic!

GLASS OF ICE

We went to a new restaurant that had just opened in our neighborhood. Table for 6.

I asked for a ginger ale (it came in a small bottle) and a glass of ice. The waiter brought them.

I looked at the glass of ice. It looked strange.

When I looked closer, there was someone's check crumpled up in the glass under the ice.

I called the waiter over. "Can I have a different glass of ice? This one has something in it."

The waiter looked at the glass. "I am so sorry," he said. "I don't know how I could have missed that."

He left to get me another glass of ice.

I said to our dinner mates, "I'm just glad I didn't pour my bottle of ginger ale into the glass of ice and then drink it!"

We all ordered appetizers.

My one friend ordered an appetizer, but the waiter brought him a different one.

They had a tough opening month.

But we've been back to that restaurant several times since, and it appears that they now have their act together.

SAME ORTHOPEDIST

I've been in a tennis game for many years. Players have come and gone, and some have retired and moved away.

But I'm still there.

Last year, there were 8 of us. This year there are 10 of us, with many new players.

At the end of last year my elbow was bothering me. One of my tennis partners told me to see a specific doctor at a well-known orthopedic institute. This doctor was an elbow expert and had helped my partner years ago.

I made an appointment. The doctor said that I didn't need surgery (yes, a surgeon said that!). He said that I had tennis elbow, and it would heal itself, with some exercises. It just takes a long while! He was right. My elbow bothered me all through last year's contract time, and it still hurts.

I later found out that 2 other players were seeing the same doctor for the same problem.

That makes 4 of the 8 players in last year's group who saw the same orthopedist.

What are the odds?

I now consider him to be our team doctor!

THE CABLE TV BILL

The bill for our cable TV was always the same amount. For several years, I made sure each month. However, I was never sure what the bill was for. It was so complicated that it was almost impossible to understand. So I decided to call our cable TV provider for an explanation.

They explained that the bill included the cost of several high-definition boxes. I had one less than their number.

I looked back over my bills, and this had been going on for at least 4 years! It was $9.95 per month for the extra box, plus taxes and fees. A total of $11.37 each month. When I added them up, the overcharges were over $500!

I requested that they refund all the overcharges.

I couldn't believe what happened next. The cable provider said that they will only correct the bill for 6 months back. That was under $70!

I had to eat the overcharges for all those months prior to 6 months back (over $400).

Rule #1.

So check your monthly bills when they come in, and make sure you understand what they are billing you for. You may have a limit on how many months you have to claim a correction.

THE OVEN

It was the Thanksgiving holiday. Their kids were coming over, and they were bringing the food.

Everything was done. The table was set. The place was cleaned. Everyone was waiting.

Then it was time.

The kids arrived, and they were carrying many food items. A large turkey. A salad. Bowls of vegetables. It promised to be a wonderful Thanksgiving dinner.

The kids marched into the house and put the food on the counter in the kitchen.

Then the daughter-in-law turned on the oven.

"No!" the father yelled.

He quickly ran over and turned off the oven.

"That's my file cabinet!" he screamed.

He opened the oven door, and there were all his files.

His wife never used the oven, so what better place to store his files.

Told to me during a Thanksgiving holiday dinner.

THE SALES MISHAPS

It was a Black Friday weekend. The stores were all advertising big savings for this notorious weekend.

One department store had a sale. The newspaper said the sale was on until 3 PM on Sunday. My wife went to buy a few things at the department store. She got there at 1:30 PM on Sunday, to make sure she would finish shopping before the 3 PM deadline.

The escalators weren't working. She had to walk up. She bought things, but the cash register wasn't working. The salesgirl told her to go to another cashier. The next cashier couldn't get the drawer open. Go to the next one! The next cash register also wasn't working. Three straight cash registers!

My wife picked up a pair of gloves for 50% off, and went to pay. It was before 2:30 PM. Once again, the salesgirl told her to go to another cashier. This time there were too many customers.

It was a sale! Didn't they plan on customers?

When my wife got to the next cash register, she handed the salesman the gloves. "This is 50% off."

The salesman looked around and said, "They took the signs down. The sale is over."

It was 2:45 PM. I could visualize the steam coming out. "Look," she said. "First, your escalators didn't work. Then there were 3 straight cash registers that didn't work. And when I went to pay for these gloves, the salesgirl was too busy and sent me to you. And the sale price sign was still up!"

The salesman gave her the sale price. 50% off!

I believe he made a wise decision!

BAPTIST CHURCH SIGN

In our township there is a Baptist Church near where we live.
I was going down their street, when I saw their sign. It said,

```
Sun Worship 11:00 AM
```

It was 35°F in November. They weren't going to the beach.

I think the sign meant to say,

```
Sunday Worship 11:00 AM
```

They didn't have enough room on the electronic sign to spell out Sunday. I believe that their congregants all knew what the sign meant.

I just found it a little amusing.

THE RESORT DANCERS

We were on a vacation in the Caribbean with our daughter and her family. We stayed at a resort on the island we visited.

The resort had a show each night, and one night the show was a musical review. We went to see it. At the beginning, several singers came out and sang songs originally done by famous people. The singers captured the essence of the famous people.

Then the show dancers came out to do a dance number. They were wearing skin-tight silver-colored rubber outfits that covered them from neck to toe.

The male dancers' outfits were so tight that you could see *every*thing!

Their packages were literally on display!

One college girl was sitting with her mother in the row in front of us, and we heard her say,

"Mom, can we go now? I don't like looking at bananas."

THE MALE LION

Years ago, I saw a TV show on the National Geographic channel about lions.

The king of beasts! And how!

They discussed how a pride (a group of lions) works, and what the roles were for the female lions (the hunters) and the male lions (the protectors).

The other function for the male lion was to sire the cubs of the pride.

So the program discussed the mating habits of the pride, and showed how a male lion finds a receptive female, and then "the couple trots off into the bushes." I assumed that was it, but the camera followed the couple into the bushes!

The video went on to show how the pair mates. It took only a few seconds. Then the announcer said that the couple mated every 15 minutes for 4 days. If it's only for 12 hours a day, that's almost 200 times!

That's when the male lion became my *idol*!

The announcer then said, "At the end of the 4 days the couple emerges from the bushes, and the male lion is visibly thinner!"

Recently I saw another show on the same channel, again about lions. They again talked about the mating habits within the pride, and this time, they said that the couple mates every 20 minutes up to 40 times per day, for 5 or 6 days!

That could be up to 240 times.

In both cases, it was a lifetime packed into a few days.

It's good to be king!

LIMITED MOBILITY

We were on a two-week cruise. Along the way we had many stops and we took the offered excursions. The tour busses had the first 2 rows reserved for "Persons With Limited Mobility."

I was used to seeing the typical wheelchair symbol, indicating a place for persons with disabilities. "Persons With Limited Mobility" must be the new expression.

I would never take up a seat in such a row. So most of the time I was either in the middle of the bus or toward the back.

On one excursion, I was seated in the middle of the bus when 2 elderly people got on with their canes. They had difficulty getting to the back of the bus, and I asked the lady who walked past me first, "Why aren't you sitting in the first 2 rows?"

She answered, "Our mobility isn't limited enough."

Her husband followed right behind her with his own cane, and I said to him, "How long have you been married?"

He answered, "Sixty years."

I said, "Sit in front."

THE SCRIPT

I was seeing a doctor for other arm issues, and he thought my arm had healed up. I was discharged.

But it still hurt.

So much that it would wake me up.

I wondered if physical therapy would help.

I called the doctor's office and reached an answering service. I left a message asking if it were possible to get a script for physical therapy since my arm was still hurting. I left my cell phone number and asked that they call me back and let me know so I could schedule a physical therapy appointment.

While I was waiting for the return call from the doctor's office, I made a physical therapy appointment for the following Monday, a week later. I made the appointment since the physical therapy office is very busy, and it's difficult to get an appointment there within 1 or 2 days. I was betting on getting the script by the appointment time. If not, I would have to postpone the appointment.

After three days, I hadn't heard from the doctor's office. My physical therapy appointment was the next day, and I had to know if I should postpone.

I called the doctor's office to inquire. They told me that they had faxed the script directly to the physical therapy office on the day I called.

Would have been nice if someone *told* me!

THE REFRIGERATOR REPAIRMAN

When we moved into our condo, we bought a new refrigerator, and it worked beautifully for several years. Then the ice maker broke, so I had to call the repairman. The rest of the refrigerator was working fine.

When I called the repair place, they had an ad on their answering machine before you were connected to a live person. The ad said that if you establish a 4-hour time period for your repair (i.e. 8 AM -12 Noon on a specified day), they will give you a small credit if the repairman is late.

We established my appointment for 8 AM – 12 Noon on Tuesday of the next week, since ice wasn't an emergency. The refrigerator portion was working.

When the time for my appointment came, I got up to wait for the repairman. By 11:30, he hadn't arrived. Then the phone rang. The lady told me that the repairman wouldn't make it by 12:00 noon.

I said I couldn't extend the time since I had a dentist appointment.

She gave me the small credit and rescheduled my appointment to Thursday. When she finished entering the information in her computer, she said, "Have a nice time at the dentist."

(She actually said that.)

I replied, "Those two things, a nice time and a dentist, should never be mentioned in the same sentence."

I think the lady from the repair place is still laughing.

THE OTHER GUY

On one of our cruises, we had dinner at a sharing table. We always select sharing as our primary dining option.

For this one sharing session, the people were very nice. We talked for a while, telling each other stories and funny things that had happened.

Another female traveler was sitting 3 tables away. The other guy at our table said she was a Butterface.

"What's that?" I asked.

He said, "She has a nice body, but her face ..."

Never heard that before.

I was still laughing 2 days later.

The same fellow said he retired several years ago, and it took him a while to figure out what he was going to do in retirement.

He decided he would be a go-getter.

Then he told me his definition.

"I will take my wife somewhere, drop her off, and when she's done, I'll go get her."

THE NEW WORDS

I learn new words every day. Most of the time they're in English.

We've been going to Mexico for 15 years, and I believe I've learned 15 new Spanish words. We're going again next year, and I plan to learn another new Spanish word!

When I heard this one new word (in English), I had to ask what it meant. Now I use it as applicable.

The person said, "I'm exhaustipated."

"What does that mean?" I asked.

"It means, 'I'm so tired I don't give a s--t!'"

HIGH SCHOOL REUNIONS

35TH HIGH SCHOOL REUNION

It was my high school's 35th reunion. My high school was an all-boys school.

I was invited, as I usually was to the reunions, and I decided to go for the first time. I hadn't seen my classmates in decades.

I play tennis, and I've played with lots of people over several years.

My 35th high school reunion was held at a local downtown hotel. As I was walking in, so was one of my tennis friends. We both looked at each other as if to say,

"What are *you* doing here?"

Turns out we were both in the same class in high school. We hadn't recognized each other even though we'd been playing tennis together for almost 3 years.

That was almost 25 years ago.

Since we reconnected, we've become good friends.

Life takes funny turns.

50TH HIGH SCHOOL REUNION

At my 50th high school reunion, we had a Friday night all-boys dinner with 110 attendees, and on Saturday night, the dinner was with spouses and a band. We had 144 attendees.

The reunion committee all thought this event was well attended, since we had only 368 students who graduated 50 years earlier.

At the Friday night dinner, the class VP opened the all-boys festivities and said, "We'll pass the microphone around the room and each guy will us tell what they've been doing for 50 years. You each have 30 seconds."

One classmate took the microphone and gave the best response. "I'm a CPA. I have 2 children. My son is a lawyer and my daughter is an MD. She's not a doctor. She's a major disappointment."

Another classmate said, "I've been on the verge of divorce for the last 50 years."

He's a lawyer.

I believe he knows what he's talking about.

55TH REUNION LUNCHEON

My 55th high school reunion started on a Friday, with lunch at the high school. Dinner was held on Saturday night, again with wives and a band.

On Friday, I took my wife to the luncheon event. Several wives were there.

After the tour and presentation, we adjourned for lunch. A room was set up, and lunch was catered with sandwiches, potato salad, cole slaw, plates, cups, ice, sodas, and desserts.

But no silverware. Not even plastic.

My wife said, "This luncheon was obviously set up by a man. A woman would *never* have forgotten the silverware."

Can't argue with that!

After much consternation, the tour guides ran to the cafeteria for plastic knives and forks.

56TH HIGH SCHOOL REUNION

It was my 56th high school reunion dinner. The class was doing them every year instead of every 5 years. With all of us getting older, we couldn't afford to wait anymore.

The dinner was held at a country club, where one of my classmates was a member. He arranged everything.

There were 12 guys and our wives (not a very big attendance, like at our 50th).

One wife said, "Let the guys stand together and we'll take a picture."

We all stood and the last guy to join the group was my classmate who was short.

He said, "Where should I stand?"

I said, "Stand in front. You're short."

He said, "Instead, why don't we do it by health?"

"What do you mean," I asked.

He said, "How many pills do you take?"

We're still holding the reunion dinners every year.

The list of classmates has dwindled.

ANOTHER HIGH SCHOOL GRAD

On our last cruise, the ship had to change the itinerary due to a hurricane. There were several sea days, and my wife found several women with whom to play Mah Jongg to pass the time on those sea days.

It turned out that one woman and her husband lived near us! Then my wife found out more details. Her husband went to my high school in the class before mine. I didn't know him.

We had dinner with them and the couple they were with, several times on the 18-day cruise.

He had a PhD and he was obviously very smart.

He told me a high school story.

He and his wife took a previous cruise to Iceland. On this cruise there was a lecturer who gave lectures on sea days. My schoolmate attended his lectures.

On one of the Iceland cruise's sea days, after one of the lectures, a woman my schoolmate didn't know came up to him and asked him, "Did you go to the following high school?" She mentioned the name of our high school.

He looked at her in amazement. "How in the world would you know to ask that?" he asked.

"You ask questions just like my husband does. He went to your high school."

THE CONDO AND THE ASSOCIATION

CONDO RULES

We bought our condo in June many years ago, and we moved in at the beginning of September. Before we moved into our condo, we received the condo documents, and we read through them to make sure we were in compliance.

Then the move-in began.

During this period, the lead guard inflicted several rules on us. None of these was in the documents we had received.

Here are a few I can still remember.

1. No deliveries on weekends.
2. No carpet installation on Friday.
3. No cardboard box removal on Saturday.
4. No cardboard box removal on Sunday.

In all, there were 9 rules that weren't in the documents. It felt like the lead guard relished the idea of inflicting these unpublished rules on us.

I wrote these rules down in a complaint letter to the Management Office. This caused the Office to issue a new Owners Guide, which had the unpublished rules incorporated.

The new guide wouldn't help us, but I figured it would help anyone who bought in our building at a later time.

MOVING INTO OUR CONDO

Since we moved in 3 months after we bought the condo, we had time to redo the kitchen. I rearranged the walls and doors to give us more usable space. Now it's much better than what was there before.

We bought everything from two stores. The kitchen design and installation and 12 new kitchen cabinets from the first store, and 3 new kitchen appliances from an appliance store (we brought our previous refrigerator from the old house, with measurements). We also bought a new washer/dryer set from the appliance store.

We had everything set up to flow in order. Kitchen walls and doors completed first. Then the old kitchen cabinets removed, and the new ones installed. Then the appliances installed.

We moved all the living room furniture into the dining room so we'd have space in the living room to store the cabinets and kitchen appliances.

The condo rules were that no deliveries could be made before 8:30 AM. We set the appliance deliveries up for 8:30 AM on the Monday we moved in. We'd hold the kitchen appliances for installation.

Straightforward, right?

Then things began to happen. The appliance store's delivery people came at 7:30 AM and were turned away. They had to come back another day. It took 3 tries to get all the appliances delivered. During that time, the boxes with the new kitchen appliances went into the living room. Then the cabinets came, also placed in the living room.

When the delivery people took the washer and dryer out of their boxes, the washer had a big dent. It had to be replaced. That took 2 more deliveries.

After the kitchen walls were redone, the unthinkable happened. The first store's kitchen installation contractor didn't have enough insurance to do work in our condo building. The store had to get another contractor. We were on hold for more than a week until they found one. And all the boxes sat in our living room until they found a new contractor.

When a different kitchen contractor was found, the kitchen work could begin, starting with the old cabinet removal. A friend from work needed kitchen cabinets for his church, so he saved us some disposal money by taking the old cabinets once they were removed. Then the new cabinets could be installed.

When it was all over, it took 10 times to get everything delivered, and four months to complete the work. We lived in our bedrooms while the all this work went on.

It wasn't as straightforward as we originally thought.

THE PLEDGE

The condo we bought was on a high floor. The building manager told us to get some flashlights since if the power ever went out, it would be very dark that high up. Even if the streetlights were working, they wouldn't reach.

We got 3 flashlights, and we put the first in the right-side cabinet of the bathroom, below the countertop. The second went into our middle bedroom, and the third into the back bedroom.

One night in February, several months after we moved in, we were watching television in the living room around 9:30 PM. It was dark outside. Then it began to rain, with loud thunder in the distance. The thunder got closer and closer, until there was a loud thunderclap right above us.

At that instant the lights went out, and everything went black. I couldn't even see my wife, who was sitting right next to me.

"Do you remember where you put the flashlights?" I heard my wife ask in the dark.

"Yes. I think the closest one is in the bathroom. I'll walk slowly and feel my way down the hall until I get there."

I felt my way to the hallway and then down the hall until I got to the bathroom. Then I bent down and opened the right-side cabinet under the countertop and felt for the flashlight. I picked it up and pressed the button.

From then on, I smelled like Lemon Pledge (furniture polish spray).

TOILET WOES

After several months in the new condo, we were having trouble with one toilet. Sometimes it wouldn't flush.

Sometimes?

That didn't make sense to an engineer.

We tried many things, but nothing helped. The building maintenance people couldn't find anything wrong. But still it continued.

Finally, I called in outside plumbers. Two plumbers came to our condo. They couldn't find anything either. Then one of them said, "Why don't we take the toilet off the floor bolts and look inside?"

Sounded good to me.

The plumbers emptied the tank and took the toilet off the floor bolts. When they turned it on its side, we heard a clunk!

They looked into the opening from below and saw the problem. Before we moved in, someone (maybe a child) had flushed an audio cassette down the toilet, and it got stuck in the water trap.

The orange plastic cassette was acting like a valve, supported at opposite corners. It turned out that whenever we put toilet paper in the bowl and flushed it, the paper would catch on the unsupported cassette corners and turn it horizontal to block the channel. Whenever the bowl was filled with fluids or refuse, it worked just fine, since the cassette would remain vertical and allow things to pass.

The plumbers cleared the channel, and the toilet has worked ever since.

I still have the orange cassette in a plastic bag.

CONDO A/C

When we moved into our condo in September, the weather was getting cooler and we didn't need much air conditioning. But the following summer, it was very hot, and our air conditioner didn't work. We turned it on, but it blew hot air.

Our condo is on the second floor from the top. In buildings like ours, the top two floors have their air conditioning condensers on the roof. That's where ours was. And it wasn't working.

We went to the management office and asked to have our air conditioner fixed. The building was responsible. The head maintenance man said he would take care of it. That was in June.

By September, nothing was done. I had severe allergies back then. We complained. Still nothing. My wife turned on the unit, and hot air still came out.

When we turned on our air conditioner, our neighbors on the top floor complained that our roof condenser unit (which was above them) was making a lot of noise. After our upstairs neighbors complained to the management office, the building replaced the condenser in a very short time.

We've had air conditioning ever since.

Since I have allergies, I don't consider air conditioning as a luxury.

It's a necessity!

KITCHEN APPLIANCES

We moved into our condo almost 20 years ago, with our refrigerator from the old house. When we redid the inside of the condo, we added the other kitchen appliances, all new.

However, 9 years later, the electric range didn't work. I joked with my wife: "Lack of use?"

She didn't think that was funny.

When the repairman checked the electric range, he said, "I have good news. I know exactly what's wrong. The touch screen display needs a part."

He called around for over a half hour, but there were no parts to be found anywhere.

Turns out the manufacturers are required by law to supply replacement parts for only 7 years, with enough parts on hand to last 2 more years. After 9 years, no parts were available anywhere.

The dominoes started falling.

1. If we couldn't fix the electric range, we would need a new one.
2. Our appliances were colored almond. That color was no longer available. They had biscuit, but that wasn't even close.
3. To make sure the colors matched, we had to get all four new kitchen appliances. We selected black and chrome, since that shouldn't go out of style.

4. The new refrigerators all had more volume. To achieve this, the designers made the refrigerators 3" taller. The space above our refrigerator was only 1½".

5. We had our carpenter remove the 15" high cabinet from above the old refrigerator, and we had to replace it with a 12" high cabinet to allow installation of the new refrigerator.

6. The manufacturer still made the 12" custom cabinets. The kitchen store ordered one, but it took 8 weeks to get it. While we were waiting for the 12" cabinet, there was a large gap above the new refrigerator in our kitchen.

7. When the 12" cabinet finally came in, our carpenter installed it. This left a 1½" gap above the new refrigerator. The carpenter had to build a 1½" filler piece to fill the space.

8. When they went to install the new dishwasher, it didn't fit between the kitchen cabinets. The appliance store replaced the dishwasher with a different model that was thinner, and the carpenter still had to shave the interior cabinet walls.

9. When that dishwasher didn't work, the store replaced it with an ultra-quiet model that was much more expensive, on their own dime.

When the dust settled, we had new kitchen appliances, even though the colors had all changed.

But we had a modern look. Right?

It cost us several thousand dollars to make this upgrade, all for the lack of a part.

THE PINOCHLE GAME #1

I subbed as a fourth in my second pinochle game for several years. I knew the other 3 guys for a long time, and they were as good as the players in my first game. These 3 players decided to drive to my condo complex every time I subbed in their game.

We played at my place during the period when my wife and I were getting new appliances for the kitchen. As I described previously, we had to wait for a 12" kitchen cabinet. While we were waiting, the pinochle game was still going on, in my kitchen.

The first time we played at my house after the kitchen appliance saga began, we were sitting at my kitchen table when I asked the other three guys if they noticed anything different.

"Did you get new appliances?" they asked.

It surprised me that all 3 of them noticed!

"Yes, I did. See anything else?"

They looked around.

"I don't see anything," they each said.

The large gap where the 12" cabinet was going to be installed was still there.

I didn't mention it. They never asked what I was talking about.

We played at my place three more times before the 12" cabinet was delivered. The gap was there for every game. The three of them never said anything about the gap above the refrigerator the entire time.

I never did mention it to them.

THE PINOCHLE GAME #2

I played in a pinochle game with three neighbors. It was a good game, and we played every week.

Then the players began to pass away. All three of them. I searched around and after several years I finally found another game, where they already had four players. I was lucky enough that one of their players bought a place in Florida, and he went there for 6 months out of the year. They asked me to be a sub for their fourth.

I played with these guys as a sub for several years. At one point I told them the fate of the players in my previous game.

Then one of these players passed away. Then a second one passed away. That left only me and the third guy.

I asked him several times if this third player knew anyone else who could fill out a foursome, but he said he didn't know anyone.

Was he having second thoughts about continuing to play with me?

EMBEZZLEMENT

When I was first elected and made president many years ago, I insisted that our first act would be to protect everyone on Council by making sure no one had a chance to pilfer money.

I suggested the same system my wife had used in her job. It worked for her for almost 18 years. That's why I used it.

Our Building Manager cuts the checks but can't sign them. Council cannot cut a check. Then we need 2 Council members to sign each check, and the Building Manager has to explain why the check was cut. This system is still in place today.

After I spent 5 years as president of the building's condo association, my wife met a woman in the elevator. The woman and her husband had just moved into our condo building. My wife told the woman that I was president of the condo association. A short time later, my wife invited them to our unit for a Saturday night get-together with other couples.

Welcoming the new couple.

A nice thing to do.

When her husband walked in, I met him for the first time. I said hello, but the first thing out of his mouth was, "How do you deal with embezzlement?"

Didn't his wife tell him I was the president of the condo association?

CLEANING LADY IS COMING

As we got older, we decided it would be a good idea to have someone else do the hard work around the house. This way, she wouldn't have to do it.

When we sold our house and moved into our condo, we hired a new cleaning lady.

The new cleaning lady did a great job, but my wife always redid some of the things to her own liking. At least she didn't have to do the heavy lifting.

This cleaning lady has been with us from the beginning of our life in the condo. There are only two of us, so she comes every two weeks, on Tuesday.

Whenever the cleaning lady is scheduled to do our condo, my wife tells me in advance,

"It's Tuesday. The cleaning lady is coming today. Straighten up for her!"

(Sound familiar?)

FLORIDA

A friend told me that he was going to retire and move to Florida, and that he was going to die there.

I told him that if I knew I were going to die in Florida, I wouldn't go there.

Printed in the United States
By Bookmasters

Printed in the United States
By Bookmasters